Red-Eye Crocodile Skinks as Pets

Red-Eye Crocodile Skink Facts and Information.

Red-Eye Crocodile Skink Care, Behavior, Diet, Interaction, Costs and Health.

By

Ben Team

Foreword

Some reptile keepers prefer to maintain species that are easy to handle and hold. Many won't even seriously consider species that don't tolerate significant interaction.

But other keepers aren't very interested in handling their pets. They approach the hobby in a manner more consistent with aquarists, rather than those who would enjoy keeping ferrets, macaws or other pets that enjoy a lot of interaction.

Such keepers enjoy a lot more flexibility when selecting their pets. Not only can they select easily handled species, but they can also pick animals who don't tolerate or are otherwise unsuitable for very much direct contact.

One of the most exciting species available to these keepers is the red-eye crocodile skink (*Tribolonotus gracilis*). As many keepers are beginning to learn, these animals make fascinating captives, even though they are not well-suited for frequent interaction with their keeper.

Red-eye crocodile skinks are interesting and beautiful lizards, who – as their name implies – resemble small crocodiles in many respects.

They are clad in several rows of large scales, which resemble the scales along the back of crocodilians, and they have large, armored heads like their namesakes too. Red-eye crocodile skinks are also crepuscular animals, like many crocodilians.

But, unlike crocodilians, red-eye crocodile skinks are quite small. Several adults can comfortably live out their lives in a relatively small aquarium, and they only need a handful or two of insects each week for food.

However, red-eye crocodile skinks are about as tolerant of interaction as real crocodiles are. These small lizards certainly aren't dangerous, and they don't even offer bites in protest very often, but they do not enjoy being held by their keepers.

However, this isn't a problem for many keepers, who simply enjoy the lizards for their incredible appearance and the interesting behaviors they exhibit.

Additionally, because these animals aren't very commonly kept as pets (at least when compared with some other species), amateurs can occasionally contribute meaningful discoveries and observations to the hobby.

But to care for your lizards properly, you'll need to learn about their biology, behavior and maintenance requirements. You can begin doing exactly that on the following pages.

Table of Contents

About the Author

The author, Ben Team, is an environmental educator and author with over 16 years of professional reptile-keeping experience.

Ben currently maintains www.FootstepsInTheForest.com, where he shares information, narration and observations of the natural world.

PART I: THE RED-EYE CROCODILE SKINK

Properly caring for any animal requires an understanding of the species and its place in the natural world. This includes digesting subjects as disparate as anatomy and ecology, diet and geography, and reproduction and physiology.

It is only by learning what your pet is, how it lives, what it does that you can achieve the primary goal of animal husbandry: Providing your pet with the highest quality of life possible.

Chapter 1: Red-Eye Crocodile Skink Description and Anatomy

Like most other reptiles, red-eye crocodile skinks (*Tribolonotus gracilis*) have evolved a number of morphological adaptations to help them survive.

But although they certainly exhibit a few anatomical peculiarities, they possess a fairly typical body plan, which resembles that of most other lizards.

Size

Red-eye crocodile skinks are small lizards. Most adults reach lengths of between 7 and 9 inches (18 to 23 centimeters) in total length, with the tail representing about half of this length. At maturity, most red-eye crocodile skinks weigh about 1.25 to 1.5 ounces (35 to 45 grams).

Young red-eye crocodile skinks hatch at lengths ranging from 3 to 8 inches (8 to 20 centimeters) and weigh about 1/10 ounce (2 to 3 grams).

Scalation

Red-eye crocodile skinks are clad in very interesting-looking scales that are responsible to a large degree for the skinks' unusual and crocodile-like appearance.

The first thing you'll notice about the scalation of the red-eye crocodile skink is four rows of raised, fin-like scales that travel from the back of the head to the tail. They are largest anteriorly; by the time they reach mid-tail, the scales have become very small, bump-like keels.

The sides are covered in small tubercles. Those with keels are members of a closely related species, the Irian Jaya crocodile skink (*Tribolonotus novaeguineae*). The legs are covered in rough, armor-like scales.

The head scales are largely fused, which creates a helmet-like effect. The scales project from the rear of the head, which further contribute to the helmet-like appearance.

Color and Pattern

Red-eye crocodile skinks are somewhat variable in color. Most are brown, gray or black dorsally. The sides are a similar but slightly lighter shade, and the ventral surfaces vary from cream to yellow.

Note the bright orange color of this lizard's eyes.

However, the most obvious colors present on the red-eye crocodile skink are the red to orange scales that surround the eyes.

Hatchling crocodile skinks often have a light-colored stripe that runs down the back, and the head is usually light brown. These colors slowly darken over time.

Body, Head and Tail

Despite their relatively unusual appearance, red-eye crocodile skinks have a fairly normal body plan for a skink.

Red-eye crocodile skinks have large, triangular heads. The eyes are rather large (and they appear even larger, thanks to the red or orange scales surrounding them). The tympanic membranes are visible and located at the rear of the head. The nostrils are located near the end of the snout.

Red-eye crocodile skinks have four short but muscular legs, which bear five long toes. Their bodies are elongated, yet moderately thick for their size.

The tail is about half the total body length, muscular and autonomous.

Vent

Like all other lizards, red-eye crocodile skinks possess a vent at the base of their tail. Located on the ventral side of the body, the vent serves as the exit point for urates and feces. It is also the place from which the hemipenes of males and the eggs produced by females emerge.

Internal Organs

The internal anatomy of red-eye crocodile skinks differs relatively little from that of other lizards.

Red-eye crocodile skinks draw oxygen in through their nostrils; pipe it through the trachea and into the lungs. Here, blood exchanges carbon dioxide for oxygen, before it is pumped to the various body parts via the heart and blood vessels.

While the hearts of red-eye crocodile skinks feature only three true chambers (two atria and a single ventricle), a septum keeps the ventricle divided at most times, allowing the heart to operate similarly to a four-chambered, mammalian heart.

This means that in practice, red-eye crocodile skinks keep their oxygenated and deoxygenated blood relatively separate in the heart.

Their digestive system is comprised of an esophagus, stomach, small intestine, large intestine and a terminal chamber called the cloaca. The stomach has some ability to stretch and accommodate food.

The liver resides near the center of the animal's torso, with the gallbladder sitting directly behind it. While the gallbladder stores bile, the liver provides a number of functions relating to digestion, metabolism and filtration.

Kidneys, which lie almost directly behind the lungs, filter wastes from the bloodstream.

Like other lizards, red-eye crocodile skinks control their bodies via their brain and nervous system. Their endocrine and exocrine glands work much as they do in other vertebrates.

Reproductive Organs
Like all squamates, red-eye crocodile skinks have paired reproductive organs, called hemipenes. When not in use, males keep their hemipenes inside the bases of their tails. When they attempt to mate with a female, they evert one of the hemipenes and insert it into the female's cloaca.

The paired nature of the male sex organs ensures that males can continue to breed if they suffer an injury to one of the hemipenes. This paired arrangement also allows male red-eye crocodile skinks to mate with females on either side of their body.

Females have paired ovaries, which produce ova (eggs), and they have paired oviducts, which store the eggs after they are released from the ovaries. However, only the right oviduct is functional. This means eggs released from the left ovary must travel across the body cavity to reach a working oviduct.

Accordingly, red-eye crocodile skinks produce one egg at a time (they may deposit four to six eggs over the course of the breeding season). The egg is shelled and held inside the oviduct until it is time for egg deposition. At this time, the egg is passed from the oviduct into the cloaca and out of the body via the vent.

Chapter 2: Red-Eye Crocodile Skink Biology and Behavior

Red-eye crocodile skinks exhibit a number of biological and behavioral adaptations that allow them to survive in their natural habitats.

Shedding

Like other scaled reptiles, red-eye crocodile skinks shed their old skin to reveal new, fresh skin underneath.

Shedding may occur as often as every two to four weeks or as infrequently as twice as year. The rate at which a lizard sheds largely depends on its growth rate, although stress, illness and injury may also trigger rapid shed cycles.

Unlike snakes, which tend to shed in one long piece, red-eye crocodile skinks typically shed in several small pieces. Most red-eye crocodile skinks exhibit the boldest coloration immediately following a shed.

Metabolism and Digestion

Red-eye crocodile skinks are ectothermic ("cold-blooded") animals, whose internal metabolism depends on their body temperature. When warm, their bodily functions proceed more rapidly; when cold, their bodily functions proceed slowly.

This also means that the lizards digest more effectively at suitably warm temperatures than they do at suboptimal temperatures. Their appetites also vary with temperature, and if the temperatures drop below the preferred range, they may cease feeding entirely.

A red-eye crocodile skink's body temperature largely follows ambient air temperatures. They try to keep their body temperature within the preferred range by moving through the habitat while exploiting microhabitats of varying temperatures.

However, red-eye crocodile skinks are not thought to bask often, if at all.

Growth Rate and Lifespan

Red-eye crocodile skinks have a relatively slow growth rate. Although the rate of growth varies according to a litany of factors – including species, sex, food availability and health – most take about 3 to 4 years to reach maturity.

Little is known about the lifespan of wild-living red-eye crocodile skinks. However, several captives have lived for longer than 5 years. As with most other small to medium-sized lizards, many probably perish at the hands of predators before reaching their first birthday.

Foraging Behavior

Red-eye crocodile skinks actively forage for prey. They typically prowl through the leaf litter or coconut husk piles on plantations, where they seek out soft-bodied arthropods.

Little is known about the specific prey preferences of hunting behavior of these secretive and poorly known lizards.

Red-eye crocodile skinks are capable of climbing, but they rarely do so.

Diel and Seasonal Activity

Red-eye crocodile skinks are crepuscular animals, who become most active at dawn and dusk. They are rarely active during the middle of the day or the middle of the night.

Red-eye crocodile skinks remain active all year long, as the temperatures remain relatively warm year-round. However, the temperatures are slightly warmer during the rainy season, which lasts from November to March.

Defensive Strategies and Tactics

Remaining out-of-sight is the first method by which red-eye crocodile skinks seek to defend themselves. They spend much of their time under some type of cover, such as leaf litter or decaying logs.

If caught in the open, they typically rely on crypsis for protection. Their earth-tone colors and rough scales help to break up their body shape and blend in quite well in their natural habitats.

However, if grasped by a predator, red-eye crocodile skinks may employ a unique defense strategy: They may emit vocalizations. These vocalizations may startle the predator, causing it to drop the lizard.

Additionally, young red-eye crocodile skinks often play dead and remain motionless if picked up.

Reproduction

Red-eye crocodile skinks breed in the wet season, which lasts from November to March. Most of the details of courtship and mating remain unknown and likely occur in secluded areas, such as burrows or beneath the leaf litter.

Females deposit eggs singly, about six weeks apart from each other. Once egg deposition has occurred, the females (and often, the males) will guard the eggs and defend them from predators.

The eggs hatch in about 70 days, although the precise duration of the incubation period can vary slightly. The young may live near their parents for an extended period of time, although it doesn't appear as though any care is provided.

Chapter 3: Classification and Taxonomy

Like all other living species, red-eye crocodile skinks are placed within a hierarchical classification scheme. The highest levels of this classification scheme help distinguish groups like vertebrates from others, while the lower levels of classification distinguish red-eye crocodile skinks from other lizards.

As currently construed, the red-eye crocodile skink's classification scheme is as follows:

Kingdom: Animalia

Phylum: Chordata

Class: Reptilia

Order: Squamata

Family: Scincidae

Genus: *Tribolonotus*

Species: *gracilis*

No subspecies of the red-eye crocodile skink are currently recognized.

Note that the closely related spiny skink (*Tribolonotus novaeguineae*) generally resembles the red-eye crocodile skink, and it is sometimes sold under the same name.

Both species are very similar, but the spiny skink has keeled scales on its sides, rather than the tubercle-like scales on the sides of red-eye crocodile skinks.

Chapter 4: The Red-Eye Crocodile Skink's World

Red-eye crocodile skinks have a relatively restricted range, and they are only found in a handful of different habitat types within this range.

Range

Red-eye crocodile skinks are primarily located on the island of New Guinea, including parts of Papua New Guinea and Indonesia (Irian Jaya). They are also found on the Admiralty Islands and likely many other small offshore islands within close proximity to New Guinea's shores.

Although rare, red-eye crocodile skinks occasionally climb.

Other species in the genus Tribolonotus inhabit other nearby islands, including the Solomon Islands and the Bismarck Archipelago.

Climate and Habitat

Red-eye crocodile skinks have historically inhabited the tropical forests of New Guinea. Unusually for lizards, they tend to prefer cool, shaded stream valleys, where the temperatures are often cooler than the surrounding area.

However, they've recently been documented inhabiting piles of discarded coconut husks and other areas near plantations. These plantations have replaced large swaths of the tropical forests that formerly covered the region, so the skinks are likely adapting to the shifting landscape.

While the temperatures in the surrounding areas may exceed 90 degrees Fahrenheit (32 degrees Celsius) during the middle of the day, the temperatures within red-eye crocodile skink habitats typically range from about 82 degrees Fahrenheit (27 degrees Celsius) during the middle of the day to about 72 degrees Fahrenheit (22 degrees Celsius) at night.

Although the temperatures remain fairly consistent throughout the year, they may rise slightly higher than normal during the wet season, which typically lasts from November to March.

PART II: RED-EYE CROCODILE SKINK HUSBANDRY

Once equipped with a basic understanding of what red-eye crocodile skinks *are* (Chapter 1 and Chapter 3), where they *live* (Chapter 4), and what they *do* (Chapter 2) you can begin learning about their captive care.

Animal husbandry is an evolving pursuit. Keepers shift their strategies frequently as they incorporate new information and ideas into their husbandry paradigms.

There are few "right" or "wrong" answers, and what works in one situation may not work in another. Accordingly, you may find that different authorities present different, and sometimes conflicting, information regarding the care of these lizards.

In all cases, you must strive to learn as much as you can about your pet and its natural habitat, so that you may provide it with the best quality of life possible.

Chapter 5: Red-Eye Crocodile Skinks as Pets

Red-eye crocodile skinks can make rewarding pets, but you learn all you can about them before adding one to your home. This includes not only understanding the nature of the care they require but also the costs associated with this care.

Assuming that you feel confident in your ability to care for a red-eye crocodile skink and endure the associated financial burdens, you can begin seeking your individual pet.

Understanding the Commitment

Keeping a red-eye crocodile skink as a pet requires a substantial commitment. You will be responsible for your pet's well-being for the rest of its life. Red-eye crocodile skink often live for 5 years or more, and you must be prepared to care for your new pet for this entire time.

Can you be sure that you will still want to care for your pet several years in the future? Do you know what your living situation will be? What changes will have occurred in your family? How will your working life have changed over this time?

You must consider all of these possibilities before acquiring a new pet. Failing to do so often leads to apathy, neglect and even resentment, which is not good for you or your pet red-eye crocodile skink.

Neglecting your pet is wrong, and in some locations, a criminal offense. You must continue to provide quality care for your red-eye crocodile skink, even once the novelty has worn off, and it is no longer fun to clean the cage and provide him with insects each week.

Once you purchase a red-eye crocodile skink, its well-being becomes your responsibility until it passes away at the end of a long life, or you have found someone who will agree to adopt the animal for you. Unfortunately, this is rarely an easy task. You may begin with thoughts of selling your pet to help recoup a small part of your investment, but these efforts will largely fall flat.

While professional breeders may profit from the sale of red-eye crocodile skinks, amateurs are at a decided disadvantage. Only a tiny sliver of the general population is interested in reptilian pets, and only a small subset of these are interested in keeping red-eye crocodile skinks.

Of those who are interested in acquiring a red-eye crocodile skink, most would rather start fresh, by *purchasing* a small hatchling or juvenile from an established breeder, rather than adopting your questionable animal *for free.*

After having difficulty finding a willing party to purchase or adopt your animal, many owners try to donate their pet to a local zoo. Unfortunately, this rarely works either.

Zoos are not interested in your red-eye crocodile skink, no matter how pretty he is. He is a pet with little to no reliable provenance and questionable health status. This is simply not the type of animal zoos are eager to add to their multi-million-dollar collections.

Zoos obtain most of their animals from other zoos and museums; failing that, they obtain their animals directly from their land of origin. As a rule, they do not accept donated pets.

No matter how difficult it becomes to find a new home for your unwanted red-eye crocodile skink, you must never release non-native reptiles into the wild.

The Costs of Captivity

Reptiles are often marketed as low-cost pets. While true in a relative sense (the costs associated with dog, cat, horse or tropical fish husbandry are often much higher than they are for red-eye crocodile skinks), potential keepers must still prepare for the financial implications of reptile ownership.

At the outset, you must budget for the acquisition of your pet, as well as the costs of purchasing or constructing a habitat. Unfortunately, while many keepers plan for these costs, they typically fail to consider the on-going costs, which will quickly eclipse the initial startup costs.

Startup Costs

One surprising fact most new keepers learn is the enclosure and equipment will often cost as much as (or more than) the animal does (except in the case of very high-priced specimens).

Prices fluctuate from one market to the next, but in general, the least you will spend on a healthy red-eye crocodile skink is about $100 (£70); you'll also need to spend another $50 (£36) on his initial habitat and care equipment. Replacement equipment and food will represent additional (and ongoing) expenses.

Ongoing Costs

The ongoing costs of red-eye crocodile skink ownership primarily fall into one of three categories: food, maintenance and veterinary care.

Food costs are the most significant of the three, but they are relatively consistent and somewhat predictable. Some maintenance costs are easy to calculate, but things like equipment malfunctions are impossible to predict with any certainty. Veterinary expenses are hard to predict and vary wildly from one year to the next.

Food Costs

Food is the single greatest ongoing cost you will experience while caring for your red-eye crocodile skink. To obtain a reasonable estimate of your yearly food costs, you must consider the number of meals you will feed your pet per year and the cost of each meal.

The amount of food your red-eye crocodile skink will consume will vary based on numerous factors, including his size, the average temperatures in his habitat and his health.

As a ballpark number, you should figure that you'll need about $2 (£1.50) per week – roughly $100 (£70) per year -- for food. You could certainly spend more or less than this, but that is a reasonable estimate for back-of-the-envelope calculations.

Veterinary Costs

While you should always seek veterinary advice at the first sign of illness, it is probably not wise to haul your healthy red-eye crocodile skink to the vet's office for no reason – they don't require "checkups" or annual vaccinations as some other pets may. Accordingly, you shouldn't incur any veterinary expenses unless your pet falls ill.

However, veterinary care can become very expensive, very quickly. In addition to a basic exam or phone consultation, your red-eye crocodile skink may need cultures, x-rays or other diagnostic tests performed. In light of this, wise keepers budget at least $200 to $300 (£160 to £245) each year to cover any emergency veterinary costs.

Maintenance Costs

It is important to plan for both routine and unexpected maintenance costs. Commonly used items, such as paper towels, disinfectant and topsoil are rather easy to calculate. However, it is not easy to know how many burned out light bulbs, cracked misting units or faulty thermostats you will have to replace in a given year.

Those who keep their red-eye crocodile skinks in simple enclosures will find that about $50 (£40) covers their yearly maintenance costs. By contrast, those who maintain elaborate habitats may spend $200 (£160) or more each year.

Always try to purchase frequently used supplies, such as light bulbs, paper towels and disinfectants in bulk to maximize your savings. It is often beneficial to consult with local reptile-keeping clubs, who often pool their resources to attain greater buying power.

Myths and Misunderstandings

Unfortunately, there are many myths and misunderstandings about red-eye crocodile skink and reptile-keeping in general. Some myths represent outdated thinking or techniques, while other myths and misunderstandings reflect the desires of keepers, rather than the reality of the situation.

Myth: *Red-eye crocodile skinks are reptiles, so they are not capable of suffering or feeling pain.*

Fact: While it is important to avoid anthropomorphizing or projecting human emotions and motivations to non-human entities, reptiles – including red-eye crocodile skinks – feel pain. There is no doubt that they can experience pain and seek to avoid it. While it is impossible to know exactly what a red-eye crocodile skink thinks, there is no reason to believe that they do not suffer similarly to other animals, when injured, ill or depressed.

Myth: *My red-eye crocodile skink likes to be held so he can feel the warmth of my hands.*

Fact: Generally speaking, red-eye crocodile skinks do not like to be handled or held, and you should avoid doing so whenever possible. The myth that reptiles enjoy the heat from a person's hands springs from the notion that because reptiles are "cold-blooded," and they must derive their heat from external sources, they must enjoy warmth at all times. However, this is an oversimplification of their behavior.

Myth: *Red-eye crocodile skinks are good pets for young children.*

Fact: While many reptiles, including red-eye crocodile skinks, make wonderful pets for adults, teenagers and families, they require more care than a young child can provide. The age at which a child is capable of caring for a pet will vary, but children should be about 10 to 12 years of age before they are allowed to care for their own red-eye crocodile skink. Parents must exercise prudent judgment and make a sound assessment of their child's capabilities and maturity. Children will certainly enjoy pet reptiles, but they must be cared for by someone with adequate maturity. Additionally, it is important to consider the potential for young children contracting salmonella and other pathogens from the family pet.

Myth: *If you get tired of a red-eye crocodile skink, it is easy to find a new home for it. The zoo will surely want your pet; after all, you are giving it to them free of charge! If that doesn't work, you can always just release it into the wild.*

Fact: Acquiring a pet red-eye crocodile skink is a very big commitment. If you ever decide that your pet no longer fits your family or lifestyle, you may have a tough time finding a suitable home for it. You can attempt to sell the animal, but this is illegal in some places, and often requires a permit or license to do legally.

Zoos and pet stores will be reticent to accept your pet – even at no charge – because they cannot be sure that your pet does not have an illness that could spread through their collections. A zoo may have to spend hundreds or thousands of dollars for the care, housing and veterinary care to accept your pet red-eye crocodile skink, and such things are not taken lightly.

Some people consider releasing their red-eye crocodile skink into the wild if no other accommodations can be made, but such acts are destructive, often illegal and usually a death sentence for the lizard.

Acquiring Your Red-Eye Crocodile Skink

Modern reptile enthusiasts can acquire red-eye crocodile skinks from a variety of sources, each with a different set of pros and cons.

Pet stores are one of the first places many people see red-eye crocodile skinks, and they become the de facto source of pets for many beginning keepers. While they do offer some unique benefits to prospective keepers, pet stores are not always the best place to purchase a pet reptile; so, consider all of the available options, including breeders and reptile swap meets, before making a purchase.

Pet Stores

Pet stores offer a number of benefits to keepers shopping for red-eye crocodile skinks, including convenience: They usually stock all of the equipment your new lizard needs, including cages, heating devices and food items.

Additionally, they offer you the chance to inspect the red-eye crocodile skinks up close before purchase. In some cases, you may be able to choose from more than one specimen. Many pet stores provide health guarantees for a short period, which provide some recourse if your new pet turns out to be ill.

However, pet stores are not always the ideal place to purchase your new pet. Pet stores are retail establishments, and as such, you will usually pay more for your new pet than you would from a breeder.

Additionally, pet stores rarely know the pedigree of the animals they sell, and they will rarely know the red-eye crocodile skink's date of birth or other pertinent information.

Other drawbacks associated with pet stores primarily relate to the staff's inexperience. While some pet stores concentrate on reptiles and may educate their staff about proper red-eye crocodile skink care, many others provide incorrect advice to their customers.

It is also worth considering the increased exposure to pathogens that pet store animals endure, given the constant flow of animals through such facilities.

Reptile Expos
Reptile expos offer another option for purchasing red-eye crocodile skinks. Reptile expos often feature resellers, breeders and retailers in the same room, all selling various types of red-eye crocodile skinks and other reptiles.

Often, the prices at such events are quite reasonable and you are often able to select from many different red-eye crocodile skinks. However, if you have a problem, it may be difficult to find the seller after the event is over.

Breeders

Because they usually offer unparalleled information and support to their customers, breeders are generally the best place for most novices to shop for red-eye crocodile skinks. Additionally, breeders often know the species well and are better able to help you learn the husbandry techniques necessary for success.

The primary disadvantage of buying from a breeder is that you must often make such purchases from a distance, either by phone or via the internet. Nevertheless, most established breeders are happy to provide you with photographs of the animal you will be purchasing, as well as his or her parents.

Selecting Your Red-Eye Crocodile Skink

Not all red-eye crocodile skinks are created equally, so it is important to select a healthy individual that will give you the best chance of success.

Practically speaking, the most important criterion to consider is the health of the animal. However, the sex, age and history of the red-eye crocodile skink are also important things to consider.

Health Checklist

Always check your red-eye crocodile skink thoroughly for signs of injury or illness before purchasing it. If you are purchasing the animal from someone in a different part of the country, you must inspect it immediately upon delivery. Notify the seller promptly if the animal exhibits any health problems.

Avoid the temptation to acquire or accept a sick or injured animal in hopes of nursing him back to health. Not only are you likely to incur substantial veterinary costs while treating your new pet, you will likely fail in your attempts to restore the red-eye crocodile skink to full health. Sick animals rarely recover in the hands of novices.

Additionally, by purchasing injured or diseased animals, you incentivize poor husbandry on the part of the retailer. If retailers lose money on sick or injured animals, they will take steps to avoid this eventuality, by acquiring healthier stock in the first place and providing better care for their charges.

As much as is possible, try to observe the following features:

- **Observe the animal's skin.** It should be free of lacerations and other damage. Pay special attention to those areas that frequently sustain damage, such as the tail and the front of the face. A small cut or abrasion may be relatively easy to treat, but significant abrasions and cuts are likely to become infected and require significant treatment.

- **Gently check the animal's crevices and creases for mites and ticks**. Avoid purchasing any animal that has ectoparasites. Additionally, you should avoid purchasing any other animals from this source, as they are likely to harbor parasites as well.
- **Examine the animal's eyes and nostrils**. The eyes should not be sunken, and they should be free of discharge. The nostrils should be clear and dry – skinks with runny noses or those who blow bubbles are likely to be suffering from a respiratory infection.

- **Gently palpate the animal and ensure no lumps or anomalies are apparent**. Lumps in the muscles or abdominal cavity may indicate parasites, abscesses or tumors.

- **Observe the animal's demeanor**. Healthy red-eye crocodile skinks are aware of their environment and react to stimuli. When active, the animal should calmly explore his environment. Avoid lethargic animals, which do not appear alert.

- **Check the animal's vent**. The vent should be clean and free of smeared feces. Smeared feces can indicate parasites or bacterial infections.

The Age
Hatchling red-eye crocodile skinks are very fragile until they reach about three or four months of age. Before this, they are unlikely to thrive in the hands of beginning keepers.

Accordingly, most beginners should purchase four- or five-month-old juveniles, who have already become well established. Animals of this age tolerate the changes associated with a new home better than very young specimens do. Further, given their larger size, they will better tolerate temperature and humidity extremes than smaller animals will.

The Sex
Unless you are attempting to breed red-eye crocodile skinks, you should select a male pet, as females are more likely to suffer from reproduction-related health problems than males are.

Some females will produce and deposit (infertile) egg clutches upon reaching maturity, whether they are housed with a male or not. While this is not necessarily problematic, novices can easily avoid this unnecessary complication by selecting males as pets.

Quarantine

Because new animals may have illnesses or parasites that could infect the rest of your collection, it is wise to quarantine all new acquisitions. This means that you should keep any new animal as separated from the rest of your pets as possible. Only once you have ensured that the new animal is healthy should you introduce it to the rest of your collection.

During the quarantine period, you should keep the new red-eye crocodile skink in a simplified habitat, with a paper substrate, water bowl, several branches, basking spot and a few hiding places. Keep the temperature and humidity at ideal levels.

It is wise to obtain fecal samples from your red-eye crocodile skink during the quarantine period. You can take these samples to your veterinarian, who can check them for signs of internal parasites. Always treat any existing parasite infestations before removing the animal from quarantine.

Always tend to quarantined animals last, as this reduces the chances of transmitting pathogens to your healthy animals. Do not wash quarantined water bowls or cage furniture with those belonging to your healthy animals. Whenever possible, use completely separate tools for quarantined animals and those that have been in your collection for some time.

Always be sure to wash your hands thoroughly after handling quarantined animals, their cages or their tools. Particularly careful keepers wear a smock or alternative clothing when handling quarantined animals.

Quarantine new acquisitions for a minimum of 30 days; 60 or 90 days is even better. Many zoos and professional breeders maintain 180- or 360-day-long quarantine periods.

Chapter 6: Providing the Captive Habitat

Providing your red-eye crocodile skink with appropriate housing is and essential aspect of captive care. In essence, the habitat you provide to your pet becomes his "world."

In "the old days," those inclined to keep reptiles had few choices with regard to caging. The two primary options were to build a custom cage from scratch or construct a lid to use with a fish aquarium.

By contrast, modern hobbyists have a variety of options from which to choose. In addition to building custom cages or adapting aquaria, dozens of different cage styles are available – each with different pros and cons.

Dimensions

Throughout their lives, reptiles need a cage large enough to lay comfortably, access a range of temperatures and get enough room for exercise.

Fortunately, red-eye crocodile skinks do not require very large enclosures at all. Three square feet of space is generally sufficient for a pair of adults (and any resulting offspring), which corresponds to a 20-gallon aquarium or 3-foot-long by 1-foot-wide enclosure.

Remember, this rule is a guideline for the *minimum* amount of space your pets require. Always strive to offer the largest cage that you reasonably can. While many keepers suggest that large cages are intimidating to lizards and other reptiles, the truth is subtler. Contrary to the popular notion, large cages – in and of themselves – do not cause reptiles to experience stress.

Red-eye crocodile skinks live in habitats that exceed even the largest cages by several orders of magnitude. What they do not do, however, is spend much time exposed.

Large, barren cages that do not feature complex cage props and numerous hiding places may very well stress them. However, large, *complex* habitats afford more space for exercising and exploring in addition to allowing for the establishment of a superb thermal gradient.

In addition to total space, the layout of the cage is also important – rectangular cages are strongly preferable for a variety of reasons:

- They allow the keeper to establish more drastic heat gradients.

- Cages with one long direction allow your animals to stretch out and crawl around more than square cage do.

- Front opening cages are easier to maintain when the cages are rectangular, as you do not have to reach as far back into the cage to reach the back wall.

Aquariums

Aquariums are popular choices for skink cages, largely because of their ubiquity. Virtually any pet store that carries red-eye crocodile skinks will also stock aquariums.

Aquariums can make suitable red-eye crocodile skink cages, but they have a number of drawbacks. For starters, glass cages are hard to clean, and they are easy to break while you are carrying them around. Aquariums that are large are likely to be extremely heavy.

Aquariums are only enclosed on five sides, so keepers have to purchase or build a suitable lid for the enclosure. After-market screen tops are available, but often, they are not secure enough for escape-prone reptiles.

Commercial Cages

Commercially produced cages have a number of benefits over other enclosures. Commercial cages usually feature doors on the front of the cage, allowing them to provide better access than top-opening cages do. Additionally, bypass glass doors or framed, hinged doors are generally more secure than after-market screened lids (as are used on aquariums) are.

Additionally, plastic cages are usually produced in dimensions that make more sense for reptiles, and often have features that aid in heating and lighting the cage.

Commercial cages can be made out of wood, metal, glass or other substances, but the majority are PVC or ABS plastic.

Commercially cages are available in two primary varieties: those that are molded from one piece of plastic and those that are assembled from several different sheets. Assembled cages are less expensive and easier to construct, but molded cages have few (if any) seems or cracks in which bacteria and other pathogens can hide.

Some cage manufacturers produce cages in multiple colors. White is probably the best color for novices, as it is easy to see dirt, mites and other small problems. A single mite crawling on a white cage surface is very visible, even from a distance.

Black cages do not show dirt as well. This can be helpful for more experienced keepers who have developed proper hygiene techniques over time. Additionally, red-eye crocodile skinks often look very sharp against black cage walls.

While red-eye crocodile skinks can probably see colors, it is unlikely that cage color is a significant factor in their quality of life. If you worry about the selection of color, it is probably best to choose a dark or earth-toned color.

Plastic Storage Containers

Plastic storage containers, such as those used for shoes, sweaters or food, make suitable cages for red-eye crocodile skinks if they are customized to meet your lizards' needs. The lids for plastic storage boxes are rarely secure enough to be used for reptile maintenance without the addition of supplemental security measures.

Hobbyists and breeders overcome this by incorporating Velcro straps, hardware latches or other strategies into plastic storage container cages. While these can be secure, you must be sure they are 100 percent escape-proof before placing your pet in such cages.

The safest way to use plastic storage containers is with the use of a wooden or plastic rack. In such systems, often called "lidless" systems, the shelves of the rack form the top to the cage sitting below them. The gap between the top of the sides of the storage containers and the bottom of the shelves is usually very tight – approximately one-eighth inch or less.

When plastic containers are used, you must drill or melt numerous holes for air exchange. If you are using a lid, it is acceptable to place the holes in the lid; however, if you are using a lidless system, you will have to make the holes in the sides of the boxes.

All holes should be made from the inside towards the outside. This will help reduce the chances of leaving sharp edges inside the cage, which could cut your pets.

Homemade Cages

For keepers with access to tools and the desire and skill to use them, it is possible to construct homemade cages. However, this is not recommended for novice keepers, who do not yet have experience keeping reptiles.

A number of materials are suitable for cage construction, and each has different pros and cons. Wood is commonly used, but must be adequately sealed to avoid rotting, warping or absorbing offensive odors.

Plastic sheeting is a very good material, but few have the necessary skills, knowledge and tools necessary for cage construction. Additionally, some plastics may have extended off-gassing times.

Glass can be used, whether glued to itself or with used with a frame. Custom-built glass cages can be better than aquariums, as you can design them in dimensions that are appropriate for red-eye crocodile skinks. Additionally, they can be constructed in such a way that the door is on the front of the cage, rather than the top.

Screen Cages

Screen cages make excellent habitats for some lizards and frogs, but they are poorly suited for red-eye crocodile skinks. Screened cages simply won't maintain a high enough humidity level to keep your lizards healthy. Additionally, they are difficult to clean.

Screen cages are prone to developing week spots that can allow red-eye crocodile skinks to push through and escape.

Chapter 7: Heating the Habitat

Providing the proper thermal environment is one of the most important aspects of reptile husbandry. As ectothermic ("cold-blooded") animals, red-eye crocodile skinks rely on the surrounding temperatures to regulate the rate at which their metabolism operates.

Providing a proper thermal environment can mean the difference between a healthy, thriving pet and one who spends a great deal of time at the veterinarian's office, battling infections and illness.

While individuals may demonstrate slightly different preferences, and different species have slightly different preferences, red-eye crocodile skinks prefer ambient temperatures in the high-70s to low-80s Fahrenheit (between 25 and 27 degrees Celsius). Inactive (sleeping) red-eye crocodile skinks prefer temperatures in the low 70s Fahrenheit (21 to 23 degrees Celsius).

Red-eye crocodile skinks don't appear to bask very much, but many hobbyists find it helpful to provide a slightly warmer basking spot in the habitat. The basking spot's temperature should be around 85 degrees Fahrenheit (29 degrees Celsius).

Providing your red-eye crocodile skink with a suitable thermal environment requires the correct approach, the correct heating equipment and the tools necessary for monitoring the thermal environment.

Size-Related Heating Concerns

Before examining the best way to establish a proper thermal environment, it is important to understand that your lizard's body size influences the way in which he heats up and cools off.

Because volume increases more quickly than surface area does with increasing body size, small individuals experience more rapid temperature fluctuations than larger individuals do.

Accordingly, it is imperative to protect small individuals from temperature extremes. Conversely, larger red-eye crocodile skinks are more tolerant of temperature extremes than smaller individuals are (though they should still be protected from temperature extremes).

Thermal Gradients

In the wild, red-eye crocodile skinks move between different microhabitats so that they can maintain ideal body temperature as much as possible.

The best way to do this is by clustering the heating devices at one end of the habitat, thereby creating a basking spot (the warmest spot in the enclosure).

The temperatures will slowly drop with increasing distance from the basking spot, which creates a *gradient* of temperatures. Barriers, such as branches and vegetation, also help to create shaded patches, which provide additional thermal options.

This mimics the way temperatures vary from one small place to the next in your pet's natural habitat. By establishing a gradient in the enclosure, your captive red-eye crocodile skink will be able to access a range of different temperatures, which will allow him to manage his body temperature just as his wild counterparts do.

Adjust the heating device until the surface temperatures at the basking spot are about 85 degrees Fahrenheit (29 degrees

Celsius). Provide a slightly cooler basking spot for immature individuals.

Because there is no heat source at the other end of the cage, the ambient temperature will gradually fall as your lizard moves away from the heat source. Ideally, the cool end of the cage should be in the low 70s Fahrenheit (22 degrees Celsius).

The need to establish a thermal gradient is one of the most compelling reasons to use a roomy cage. In general, the larger the cage, the easier it is to establish a suitable thermal gradient.

Heating Equipment

There are a variety of different heating devices you can use to keep your red-eye crocodile skink's habitat within the appropriate temperature range.

Be sure to consider your choice carefully and select the best type of heating device for you and your pet.

Heat Lamps

Heat lamps are usually the best choice for supplying heat to your pet's habitat. Heat lamps consist of a reflector dome and an incandescent bulb. The light bulb produces heat (in addition to light) and the metal reflector dome directs the heat to a spot inside the cage.

You will need to clamp the lamp to a stable anchor or part of the cage's frame. Always be sure that the lamp is securely attached and will not be dislodged by vibration, children or pets.

Because fire safety is always a concern, and many keepers use high-wattage light bulbs, opt for heavy-duty reflector domes with ceramic bases, rather than economy units with plastic bases. The price difference is negligible, given the stakes.

One of the greatest benefits of using heat lamps to maintain the temperature of your pet's habitat is the flexibility they offer. While you can adjust the amount of heat provided by heat tapes and other devices with a rheostat or thermostat, you can adjust the enclosure temperature provided by heat lamps in two ways:

- Changing the Bulb Wattage

The simplest way to adjust the temperature of your pet's cage is by changing the wattage of the bulb you are using.

For example, if a 40-watt light bulb is not raising the temperature of the basking spot high enough, you may try a 60-watt bulb. Alternatively, if a 100-watt light bulb is elevating the cage temperatures higher than are appropriate, switching to a 60-watt bulb may help.

- Adjusting the Distance between the Heat Lamp and the Basking Spot

The closer the heat lamp is to the cage, the warmer the cage will be. If the habitat is too warm, you can move the light farther from the enclosure, which should lower the basking spot temperatures slightly.

However, the farther away you move the lamp, the larger the basking spot becomes. It is important to be careful that you do not move it too far away, which will reduce the effectiveness of the thermal gradient by heating the enclosure too uniformly. In very large cages, this may not compromise the thermal gradient very much, but in a small cage, it may eliminate the "cool side" of the habitat.

In other words, if your heat lamp creates a basking spot that is roughly 1-foot in diameter when it is 1 inch away from the screen, it will produce a slightly cooler, but larger basking spot when moved back another 6 inches or so.

Ceramic Heat Emitters

Ceramic heat emitters are small inserts that function similarly to light bulbs, except that they do not produce any visible light – they only produce heat.

Ceramic heat emitters are used in reflector-dome fixtures, just as heat lamps are. The benefits of such devices are numerous:

- They typically last much longer than light bulbs do

- They are suitable for use with thermostats

- They allow for the creation of overhead basking spots, as lights do

- They can be used day or night

However, the devices do have three primary drawbacks:

- They are very hot when in operation

- They are much more expensive than light bulbs

- You cannot tell by looking if they are hot or cool. This can be a safety hazard – touching a ceramic heat emitter while it is hot is likely to cause serious burns.

Radiant Heat Panels

Quality radiant heat panels are a great choice for heating most reptile habitats, including those containing red-eye crocodile skinks. Radiant heat panels are essentially heat pads that stick to the roof of the habitat. They usually feature rugged, plastic or metal casings and internal reflectors to direct the infrared heat back into the cage.

Radiant heat panels have a number of benefits over traditional heat lamps and under tank heat pads:

- They do not produce visible light, which means they are useful for both diurnal and nocturnal heat production. They can be used in conjunction with fluorescent light fixtures during the day and remain on at night once the lights go off.

- They are inherently flexible. Unlike many devices that do not work well with pulse-proportional thermostats, most radiant heat panels work well with on-off and pulse-proportional thermostats.

The only real drawback to radiant heat panels is their cost: radiant heat panels often cost about two to three times the price of light- or heat pad-oriented systems. However, many radiant heat panels outlast light bulbs and heat pads, a fact that offsets their high initial cost over the long term.

Heat Pads
Heat pads are an attractive option for many new keepers, but they are not without drawbacks.

- Heat pads have a high risk of causing contact burns.

- If they malfunction, they can damage the cage as well as the surface on which they are placed.

- They are more likely to cause a fire than heat lamps or radiant heat panels are.

However, if installed properly (which includes allowing fresh air to flow over the exposed side of the heat pad) and used in conjunction with a thermostat, they can be reasonably safe. With heat pads, it behooves the keeper to purchase premium products, despite the small increase in price.

Heat Tape
Heat tape is somewhat akin to a "stripped down" heat pad. In fact, most heat pads are simply pieces of heat tape that have already been connected and sealed inside a plastic envelope.

Heat tape is primarily used to heat large numbers of cages simultaneously. It is generally inappropriate for novices and requires the keeper to make electrical connections. Additionally, a thermostat is always required when using heat tape.

Historically, heat tape was used to keep water pipes from freezing – not to heat reptile cages. While some commercial heat tapes have been designed specifically for reptiles, many have not. Accordingly, it may be illegal, not to mention dangerous, to use heat tapes for purposes other than for which they are designed.

Heat Cables
Heat cables are similar to heat tape, in that they heat a long strip of the cage, but they are much more flexible and easy to use. Many heat cables are suitable to use inside the cage, while others are designed for use outside the habitat.

Always be sure to purchase heat cables that are designed to be used in reptile cages. Those sold at hardware stores are not appropriate for use in a cage.

Heat cables must be used in conjunction with a thermostat, or, at the very least, a rheostat.

Nocturnal Temperatures
Because red-eye crocodile skinks easily tolerate temperatures in the low-70s Fahrenheit (21 to 22 degrees Celsius) at night, most keepers can allow their pet's habitat to fall to ambient room temperature at night.

Because it is important to avoid using lights on your lizard's habitat at night, those living in homes with lower nighttime temperatures will need to employ additional heat sources. Most such keepers accomplish this through the use of ceramic heat emitters.

Thermometers

It is important to monitor the cage temperatures very carefully to ensure your pet stays healthy. Just as a water test kit is an aquarist's best friend, quality thermometers are some of the most important husbandry tools for reptile keepers.

Ambient and Surface Temperatures

Two different types of temperature are relevant for pet red-eye crocodile skinks: ambient temperatures and surface temperatures.

The ambient temperature in your animal's enclosure is the air temperature; the surface temperatures are the temperatures of the objects in the cage. Both are important to monitor, as they can differ widely.

Measure the cage's ambient temperatures with a digital thermometer. An indoor-outdoor model will feature a probe that allows you to measure the temperature at both ends of the thermal gradient at once. For example, you may position the thermometer at the cool side of the cage but attach the remote probe to a branch near the basking spot.

Because standard digital thermometers do not measure surface temperatures well, use a non-contact, infrared thermometer for such measurements. These devices will allow you to measure surface temperatures accurately from a short distance away.

Thermostats and Rheostats

Some heating devices, such as heat lamps, are designed to operate at full capacity for the entire time that they are turned on. Such devices should not be used with thermostats – instead, care should be taken to calibrate the proper temperature by tweaking the bulb wattage.

Other devices, such as heat pads, heat tape and radiant heat panels are designed to be used with a regulating device, such as a thermostat or rheostat, which maintains the proper temperature

Rheostats

Rheostats are similar to light-dimmer switches, and they allow you to reduce the output of a heating device. In this way, you can dial in the proper temperature for the habitat.

The drawback to rheostats is that they only regulate the amount of power going to the device – they do not monitor the cage temperature or adjust the power flow automatically. In practice, even with the same level of power entering the device, the amount of heat generated by most heat sources will vary over the course of the day.

If you set the rheostat so that it keeps the cage at the right temperature in the morning, it may become too hot by the middle of the day. Conversely, setting the proper temperature during the middle of the day may leave the morning temperatures too cool.

Care must be taken to ensure that the rheostat controller is not inadvertently bumped or jostled, causing the temperature to rise or fall outside of healthy parameters.

Thermostats

Thermostats are similar to rheostats, except that they also feature a temperature probe that monitors the temperature in the cage (or under the basking source). This allows the thermostat to adjust the power going to the device as necessary to maintain a predetermined temperature.

For example, if you place the temperature probe under a basking spot powered by a radiant heat panel, the thermostat will keep the temperature relatively constant at the basking site.

There are two different types of thermostats:

- On-Off Thermostats

On-Off Thermostats work by cutting the power to the device when the probe's temperature reaches a given temperature. For example, if the thermostat were set to 85 degrees Fahrenheit (29 degrees Celsius), the heating device would turn off whenever the temperature exceeds this threshold. When the temperature falls below 85, the thermostat restores power to the unit, and the heater begins functioning again. This cycle will continue to repeat, thus maintaining the temperature within a relatively small range.

Be aware that on-off thermostats have a "lag" factor, meaning that they do not turn off when the temperature reaches a given temperature. They turn off when the temperature is a few degrees above that temperature, and then turn back on when the temperate is a little below the set point. Because of this, it is important to avoid setting the temperature at the limits of your pet's acceptable range. Some premium models have an adjustable amount of threshold for this factor, which is helpful.

- Pulse Proportional Thermostats

Pulse proportional thermostats work by constantly sending pulses of electricity to the heater. By varying the rate of pulses, the amount of energy reaching the heating devices varies. A small computer inside the thermostat adjusts this rate to match the set-point temperature as measured by the probe. Accordingly, pulse proportional thermostats maintain much more consistent temperatures than on-off thermostats do.

Lights should not be used with thermostats, as the constant flickering may stress your pet. Conversely, heat pads, heat tape, radiant heat panels and ceramic heat emitters should always be used with either a rheostat or, preferably, a thermostat to avoid overheating your pet.

Thermostat Failure

If used for long enough, all thermostats eventually fail. The question is will yours fail today or twenty years from now. While some thermostats fail in the "off" position, a thermostat that fails in the "on" position may overheat your lizard. Unfortunately, tales of entire collections being lost to a faulty thermostat are too common.

Accordingly, it behooves the keeper to acquire high-quality thermostats. Some keepers use two thermostats, connected in a series arrangement. By setting the second thermostat (the "backup thermostat") a few degrees higher than the setting used on the "primary thermostat," you safeguard yourself against the failure of either unit.

In such a scenario, the backup thermostat allows the full power coming to it to travel through to the heating device, as the temperature never reaches its higher set-point temperature.

However, if the first unit fails in the "on" position, the second thermostat will keep the temperatures from rising too high. The temperature will rise a few degrees in accordance with the higher set-point temperature, but it will not get hot enough to harm your pets.

If the backup thermostat fails in the "on" position, the first thermostat retains control. If either fails in the "off" position, the temperature will fall until you rectify the situation, but a brief exposure to relatively cool temperatures is unlikely to be fatal.

Chapter 8: Lighting the Enclosure

Lighting is a contentious and controversial subject among lizard keepers. The topic most commonly comes up among keepers of diurnal lizard species, such as bearded dragons (*Pogona vitticeps*), monitor lizards (*Varanus* spp.) and various iguanas (*Iguana* spp.), but red-eye crocodile skink keepers debate the subject too.

Diurnal lizards often have very specific light requirements, which the sun meets (and greatly exceeds) with ease yet are difficult to replicate with light bulbs. Accordingly, there is a great deal such keepers must understand about light to make sure they meet their pet's needs.

However, most nocturnal and crepuscular species, such as red-eye crocodile skinks, are assumed to prefer dim cages. As a rule, they are not thought to have the same lighting requirements that most diurnal lizards do.

Most red-eye crocodile skink keepers elect not to provide any lighting for their pets (aside from that which is designed to produce heat), while others feel that sun-mimicking lights are helpful for their lizards and include them in their pet's habitat. You'll just have to learn as much as you can about the subject and make the best decision possible.

Light for Viewing

Even if you don't think that full-spectrum lighting is necessary for your lizard's health, you may want to use some form of lighting to help make your red-eye crocodile skink and his habitat easier to view.

But you must realize that, as a crepuscular lizard, your red-eye crocodile skink probably won't come out very often while the lights are on. Nevertheless, there is nothing wrong with providing some low-level lighting for your lizard's habitat.

If you use a heat lamp to provide a thermal gradient, the light from the bulb will provide more than enough illumination to appreciate your pet's habits and habitat.

But you can also add a fluorescent fixture to your pet's cage to illuminate it. An ordinary fluorescent bulb will suffice for this purpose, but you can also select a premium model, designed to produce more balanced light. This will make the colors in the cage more appealing, and it may help your plants to stay healthier.

You can also use a red-colored light at night. This will allow you to observe your lizard as he hunts and forages during his active period, but it won't disturb him, either.

In all cases, it is important to ensure that these additional lights do not raise the cage temperature above your target zone.

Light for Health

As stated earlier, most keepers believe that full-spectrum lighting is unnecessary for the maintenance of crepuscular lizards. In fact, it probably carries some risks. Strong UV rays may be able to harm the skin of sensitive reptiles, and it may alter vitamin D metabolism in undesired ways.

In practice, red-eye crocodile skinks will likely hide from the light – in fact, all reptiles housed in cages with UV-producing lights should be offered shade from the lights in at least some portion of the cage. Many reptiles are capable of seeing UV rays, and some "dose" themselves with optimal amounts of exposure. Nocturnal and crepuscular lizards probably don't require UV lighting, and most avoid bright conditions as a matter of practice.

However, those keepers who desire to include full-spectrum lighting as a component of their skink's care, or who want to understand the reasons *some* lizards require full-spectrum lighting, must first understand a little bit about light.

Light is a type of energy that physicists call electromagnetic radiation; it travels in waves. These waves may differ in amplitude, which correlates to the vertical distance between consecutive wave crests and troughs, frequency, which correlates with the number of crests per unit of time, and wavelength.

Wavelength is the distance from one crest to the next, or one trough to the next. Wavelength and frequency are inversely proportional, meaning that as the wavelength increases, the frequency decreases. It is more common for reptile keepers to discuss wavelengths rather than frequencies.

The sun produces energy (light) with a very wide range of constituent wavelengths. Some of these wavelengths fall within a range called the visible spectrum; humans can detect these rays with their eyes. Such waves have wavelengths between about 390 and 700 nanometers. Rays with wavelengths longer or shorter than these limits are broken into their own groups and given different names.

Those rays with around 390 nanometer wavelengths or less are called ultraviolet rays or UV rays. UV rays are broken down into three different categories, just as the different colors correspond with different wavelengths of visible light. UVA rays have wavelengths between 315 to 400 nanometers, while UVB rays have wavelengths between 280 and 315 nanometers while UVC rays have wavelengths between 100 and 280 nanometers.

Rays with wavelengths of less than 280 nanometers are called x-rays and gamma rays. At the other end of the spectrum, infrared rays have wavelengths longer than 700 nanometers; microwaves and radio waves are even longer.

UVA rays are important for food recognition, appetite, activity and eliciting natural behaviors in some species. UVB rays are necessary for many reptiles to produce vitamin D3. Without this vitamin, sun-dependent reptiles cannot properly metabolize their calcium.

Chapter 9: Enclosure Furniture

Strictly speaking, it is possible to keep a red-eye crocodile skink in a cage devoid of anything but a substrate that permits burrowing and a water bowl. However, it is wise to provide red-eye crocodile skinks with complex environments, containing several places to hide, burrow and explore.

Additionally, many keepers enjoy decorating the cage to resemble the animal's natural habitat. While such measures are not necessary from the lizard's point of view, if implemented with care, there is no reason not to decorate your pet's cage, if you are inclined to do so.

However, it is recommended that beginners use a simple cage design for their first 6 to 12 months while they learn to provide effective husbandry.

Hide Boxes

"Hide boxes" come in a wide variety of shapes, sizes and styles. Some keepers use modified plastic or cardboard containers, while others use realistic looking logs and wood pieces. Both approaches are acceptable, but all hides must offer a few key things:

- Hides should be safe for the lizard and feature no sharp edges or toxic chemicals.

- Hides should accommodate the lizard, but not much else. They should be only slightly larger than the animal's body.

- Hides should have low profiles. Reptiles prefer to feel the top of the hide contacting the dorsal surface of their body.

- Hides either must be easy and economical to replace or constructed from materials that are easy to clean.

Plastic Storage Boxes

Just as a plastic storage box can be converted into an acceptable enclosure, small storage boxes can be converted into functional hiding places. Food containers, shoeboxes and butter tubs can serve as the base.

If the container has a low profile, it needs only have a door cut into the tub. Alternatively, you can discard the lid, flip the tub upside down and cut an entrance hole in the side.

Plant Saucers

The saucers designed to collect the water that overfills potted plants make excellent hiding locations. All you have to do is flip them upside down and cut a small opening in the side for a door.

Clay or plastic saucers can be used, but clay saucers are hard to cut. If you punch an entrance hole into a clay saucer, you must sand or grind down the edges to prevent hurting your pet.

Plates

Plastic, paper or ceramic plates make good hiding locations in cages that use particulate substrates. This will allow the lizard to burrow up under the plate through the substrate and hide in a very tight space. Such hiding places also make it very easy to access your pet while he is hiding.

Cardboard Boxes

While you must discard and replace them anytime they become soiled, small cardboard boxes can also make suitable hide boxes. Just cut a hole in the side to provide a door.

Commercial "Half-Logs"

Many pet stores sell U-shaped pieces of wood that resemble half of a hollow log. While these are sometimes attractive looking items, they are not appropriate hide spots when used as intended.

The U-shaped construction means that the lizard will not feel the top of the hide when he is laying inside. These hides can be functional if they are partially buried, thus reducing the height of the hide.

Cork Bark

Real bark cut from the cork oak (*Quercus suber*), "cork bark" is a wonderful looking decorative item that can be implemented in a variety of ways.

Usually cork bark is available in tube shape or in flat sheets. Flat pieces are better for red-eye crocodile skinks. Flat pieces should only be used with particulate, rather than sheet-like substrates so that the lizard can get under them easily.

Cork bark may be slightly difficult to clean, as its surface contains numerous indentations and crevices. Use hot water, soap and a sturdy brush to clean the pieces.

Commercially Produced Plastic Hides

Many different manufacturers market simple, plastic, hiding boxes. These are very functional if sized correctly, although some brands tend to be too tall. The simple design and plastic construction makes them very easy to clean.

Paper Towel Tubes

Small sections of paper towel tubes make suitable hiding spots for red-eye crocodile skinks. They do not last very long, so they require frequent replacement. They often work best if flattened slightly.

Newspaper or Paper Towels

Several sheets of newspaper or paper towels placed on top of the substrate (whether sheet-like or particulate) make suitable hiding spots.

Many professional breeders use paper-hiding spaces because it is such a simple and economically feasible solution. Some keepers crumple a few of the sheets to give the stack of paper more height.

Unusual Items

Some keepers like to express their individuality by using unique or unusual items as hiding spots. Some have used handmade ceramic items, while others have used skulls or turtle shells. If the four primary criteria previously discussed are met, there is no reason such items will not make suitable hiding spaces.

Humid Hides

In addition to security, red-eye crocodile skinks also derive another benefit from many of their hiding spaces in the wild. Most hiding places feature higher humidity than the surrounding air.

By spending a lot of time in such places, red-eye crocodile skinks are able to avoid dehydration in habitats where water is scarce. Additionally, sleeping in these humid retreats aids in the shedding process. You should take steps to provide similar opportunities in captivity.

Humid hides can be made by placing damp sphagnum moss in a plastic container. The moss should not be saturated, but merely damp. You can also use damp paper towels or newspaper to increase the humidity of a hide box.

Some keepers prefer to keep humid hides in the habitat at all times, while others use them periodically – usually preceding shed cycles. Humid hides should never be the only hides available to the lizard. Always use them in addition to dry hides.

Chapter 10: Substrates

Substrates are used to give your red-eye crocodile skink a comfortable surface on which to crawl and to absorb any liquids present. There are a variety of acceptable choices, all of which have benefits and drawbacks. The only common substrate that is never acceptable is cedar shavings, which emits fumes that are toxic to reptiles.

Paper Products

The easiest and safest substrates for red-eye crocodile skinks are paper products in sheet form. While regular newspaper is the most common choice, some keepers prefer paper towels, unprinted newspaper, butcher's paper or a commercial version of these products.

Paper substrates are very easy to maintain, but they do not last very long and must be completely replaced when they are soiled. Accordingly, they must be changed regularly -- at least once per week.

Use several layers of paper products to provide sufficient absorbency and a little bit of cushion for the lizard.

Many pet stores and pet supply retailers now carry recycled paper pulp products that can be used as bedding. Many keepers have used these substrates successfully, but they don't offer the primary benefits that sheet-style paper products do.

For example, they're not as easy to replace and they represent an ingestion hazard. They also cost significantly more than a few sheets of newspaper, so they haven't become as popular as some keepers predicted.

Pine

Some hobbyists eschew pine, which is sometimes though to produce irritating fumes. While this may be true of products made from the xylem (wood) of pine trees, it is not true of products made from the bark.

Pine bark is not very absorbent, but it resists decay reasonably well. Pine bark is attractive and natural looking, but it does leave copious amounts of black dust inside the cage.

It can be spot cleaned daily but requires monthly replacement.

Orchid Bark

The bark of fir trees is often used for orchid propagation, and so it is often called "orchid bark." Orchid bark is very attractive, though not quite as natural looking as pine bark. However, it exceeds pine in most other ways except cost.

Because orchid bark is often reddish in color, it is very easy to spot clean. However, monthly replacement can be expensive for those living in the eastern United States and Europe.

Cypress Mulch

Cypress mulch is a popular substrate choice for many tropical species, and it helps to provide a high humidity level, which is often beneficial for red-eye crocodile skinks.

One significant drawback to cypress mulch is that some brands (or individual bags among otherwise good brands) produce a stick-like mulch, rather than mulch composed of thicker pieces.

These sharp sticks can injure the keeper and the kept. It usually only takes one cypress mulch splinter jammed under a keeper's fingernail to cause them to switch substrates.

Soil

Organic potting soil or soil collected from a forested area can also be used in your red-eye crocodile skink's enclosure. Both substrates are easy to acquire, affordable (or free) and retain moisture well, so they make excellent options.

Just be sure to collect the soil from an area that hasn't been exposed to pesticides or other chemicals, or, if you are purchasing the soil, opt for a variety that does not include perlite, fertilizers or other additives.

Chapter 11: Maintaining the Captive Habitat

Now that you have acquired your red-eye crocodile skink and set up the enclosure, you must develop a protocol for maintaining his habitat. While red-eye crocodile skink habitats require major maintenance every month or so, they only require minor daily maintenance.

In addition to designing a husbandry protocol, you must embrace a record-keeping system to track your red-eye crocodile skink's growth and health.

Cleaning and Maintenance Procedures

Once you have decided on the proper enclosure for your pet, you must keep your red-eye crocodile skink fed, hydrated and ensure that the habitat stays in proper working order to keep your captive healthy and comfortable.

Some tasks must be completed each day, while others are should be performed weekly, monthly or annually.

Daily
- Monitor the ambient and surface temperatures of the habitat.

- Spot clean the cage to remove any feces, urates or pieces of shed skin in the enclosure.

- Ensure that the lights, latches and other moving parts are in working order.

- Verify that your pet is acting normally and appears healthy. You do not necessarily need to handle him to do so.

Weekly
- Change sheet-like substrates (newspaper, paper towels, etc.).

- Clean the inside surfaces of the enclosure.

- Inspect your red-eye crocodile skink closely for any signs of injury, parasites or illness.

- Wash and sterilize all food dishes.

Monthly
- Break down the cage completely, remove and discard particulate substrates.

- Sterilize drip containers and similar equipment in a mild bleach solution.

- Measure and weigh your red-eye crocodile skink.

- Photograph your pet (recommended, but not imperative).

- Prune any plants present in the enclosure as necessary.

Annually
- Replace the batteries in your thermometers and any other devices that use them.

Cleaning your red-eye crocodile skink's cage and furniture is relatively simple. Regardless of the way it became soiled, the basic process remains the same:

1. Rinse the object
2. Using a scrub brush or sponge and soapy water, remove any organic debris from the object.
3. Rinse the object thoroughly.
4. Disinfect the object.
5. Re-rinse the object.
6. Dry the object.

Chemicals & Tools
A variety of chemicals and tools are necessary for reptile care. Save yourself some time by purchasing dedicated cleaning

products and keeping them in the same place that you keep your tools.

Spray Bottles
Occasionally misting your pet's cage will help ensure the enclosure doesn't become too dry. You can do this with a small, handheld misting bottle or a larger, pressurized unit (such as those used to spray herbicides). Automated units are available, but they are rarely cost-effective unless you are caring for a large colony of animals.

Small Brooms
Small brooms are great for sweeping up small messes and bits of substrate. It is usually helpful to select one that features angled bristles, as they'll allow you to better reach the nooks and crannies of your pet's cage and the surrounding area.

Ideally, the broom should come with its own dustpan to collect debris, but there are plenty of workarounds for those that don't come with their own.

Scrub Brushes or Sponges
It helps to have a few different types of scrub brushes and sponges on hand for scrubbing and cleaning different items. Use the least abrasive sponge or brush suitable for the task to prevent wearing out cage items prematurely. Do not use abrasive materials on glass or acrylic surfaces. Steel-bristled brushes work well for scrubbing coarse, wooden items, such as branches.

Spatulas and Putty Knives
Spatulas, putty knives and similar tools are often helpful for cleaning reptile cages. For example, urates (which are not soluble in anything short of hot lava) often become stuck on cage walls or furniture. Instead of trying to dissolve them with

harsh chemicals, just scrape them away with a sturdy plastic putty knife.

Small Vacuums

Small, handheld vacuums are very helpful for sucking up the dust left behind from substrates. They are also helpful for cleaning the cracks and crevices around the cage doors. A shop vacuum, with suitable hoses and attachments, can also be helpful if you have enough room to store it.

Soap

Use a gentle, non-scented dish soap. Antibacterial soap is preferred, but not necessary. Most people use far more soap than is necessary -- a few drops mixed with a quantity of water is usually sufficient to help remove surface pollutants.

Bleach

Bleach (diluted to one-half cup per gallon of water) makes an excellent disinfectant. Be careful not to spill any on clothing, carpets or furniture, as it is likely to discolor the objects.

Always be sure to rinse objects thoroughly after using bleach and be sure that you cannot detect any residual odor. Bleach does not work as a disinfectant when in contact with organic substances; accordingly, items must be cleaned before you can disinfect them.

Veterinarian Approved Disinfectant

Many commercial products are available that are designed to be safe for their pets. Consult with your veterinarian about the best product for your situation, its method of use and its proper dilution.

Avoid Phenols

Always avoid cleaners that contain phenols, as they are extremely toxic to some reptiles. In general, do not use household cleaning products to avoid exposing your pet to toxic chemicals.

A group of red-eye crocodile skinks.

Keeping Records

It is important to keep records regarding your pet's health, growth and feeding, as well as any other important details. In the past, reptile keepers would do so on small index cards or in a notebook. In the modern world, technological solutions may be easier.

You can record as much information about your pet as you like, and the more information to you record, the better. But minimally, you should record the following:

Pedigree and Origin Information

Be sure to record the source of your red-eye crocodile skink, the date on which you acquired him and any other data that is available. Breeders will often provide customers with information regarding the sire, dam, date of birth, weights and feeding records, but other sources will rarely offer comparable data.

Feeding Information

Record the date of each feeding, as well as the type of food item(s) offered. It is also helpful to record any preferences you may observe or any meals that are refused.

Weights and Length

Because you look at your pet frequently, it is difficult to appreciate how quickly he is (or isn't) growing. Accordingly, it is important to track his size diligently.

Weigh your pet with a high-quality digital scale. It is often easiest to use a dedicated "weighing container" with a known weight to measure your pet. Simply subtract the weight of the container to obtain the weight of your pet.

You can also measure your lizard's length as well, but it is not always easy to do so, as they tend to wiggle quite a bit. This can make it difficult to keep them in a straight line without putting undo pressure on their body.

However, there are a number of web-based computer applications that will calculate the length of snakes and lizards if you take and upload a photo of your pet along with something of a known length (such as a ruler).

Maintenance Information

Record all of the noteworthy events associated with your pet's care. While it is not necessary to note that you misted the cage every other day, it is appropriate to record the dates on which you changed the substrate or sterilized the cage.

Whenever you purchase new equipment, supplies or caging, note the date and source. This not only helps to remind you when you purchased the items, but it may help you track down a source for the items in the future, if necessary.

Breeding Information

If you intend to breed your red-eye crocodile skinks, you should record all details associated with pre-breeding conditioning, cycling, introductions, matings, color changes, copulations and egg deposition.

Record all pertinent information about any resulting clutches as well, including the number of viable eggs, as well as the number of unhatched and unfertilized eggs.

Chapter 12: Feeding Red-Eye Crocodile Skinks

Like most other skinks, red-eye crocodile skinks feed on invertebrates.

The best captive diet for red-eye crocodile skinks is one that mimics their wild diet, being comprised of a diverse mix of gut-loaded insects. By gut-loading your insects (feeding them nutritious fruits and vegetables before feeding the insects to your red-eye crocodile skinks) and using a diverse array of insects, you can help reduce the chances that your lizard's diet will be deficient in some area.

Nevertheless, providing a varied diet is not always sufficient to avoid deficiencies, so it is also wise to supplement some of your pet's food with vitamins and minerals.

Insects

Insects are a great food source for red-eye crocodile skinks. Crickets and very small roaches are the best commercially produced insects to offer, but very small mealworms can also be incorporated into their diet.

Some keepers supplement their captive's diet with wild caught insects, but discretion is advised, as such insects may be contaminated with pesticides or infested with parasites.

Prey Size

It is important to offer the right size insect prey, to prevent your pet from suffering injuries. As a rule of thumb, try to provide your lizard with insects that are no longer than the distance between your pet's eyes. This is especially important for small red-eye crocodile skinks, whose eyes are frequently larger than their stomach.

Feeding Quantity and Frequency

The proper feeding frequency for a red-eye crocodile skink depends on its size, species and age. Generally speaking, most red-eye crocodile skinks should be fed four to seven times per week; the younger and smaller the lizard, the more often it should be fed.

Assuming that the lizard has access to suitable temperatures and you implement an effective supplementation regimen, you aren't likely to overfeed a young red-eye crocodile skink. However, mature lizards may become overweight if fed too frequently.

Ultimately, you must adjust your lizard's diet by monitoring his weight and tail condition. Young lizards should exhibit steady, moderate growth rates, while mature animals should maintain a relatively consistent body weight throughout the year (the body weights of mature females will obviously fluctuate over the course of a breeding season, as eggs are produced and deposited).

If your lizard begins losing weight or his tail begins shrinking, you must increase the frequency of his feedings. Conversely, those that gain excessive wait should be fed slightly less food. Just be sure to consult with your veterinarian before altering your feeding schedule drastically.

Do not allow large numbers of feeder insects to roam the enclosure freely, as it can stress your pet. Additionally, the crickets may feed on the delicate skin near your lizard's eyes and vent. Only give your pet as many insects as he can eat in one sitting. Once he is full, the cage should be free of insects, or nearly so.

Vitamin and Mineral Supplements

Many keepers add commercially produced vitamin and mineral supplements to their red-eye crocodile skink's food on a regular basis. In theory, these supplements help to correct dietary deficiencies and ensure that captive lizards get a balanced diet. In practice, things are not this simple.

While some vitamins and minerals are unlikely to build up to toxic levels, others may very well cause problems if provided in excess. This means that you cannot simply apply supplements to every meal – you must decide upon a sensible supplementation schedule.

Additionally, it can be difficult to ascertain exactly how much of the various vitamins and minerals you will be providing to your lizard, as most such products are sold as fine powders, designed to be sprinkled on feeder insects.

This is hardly a precise way to provide the proper dose to your lizard, and the potential for grossly over- or under-estimating the amount of supplement delivered is very real.

Because the age, sex and health of your pet all influence the amount of vitamins and minerals your pet requires, and each individual product has a unique composition, it is wise to consult your veterinarian before deciding upon a supplementation schedule. However, most keepers provide vitamin supplementation once each week, and calcium supplementation several times per week.

Chapter 13: Providing Water to Your Red-Eye Crocodile Skink

Like most other animals, red-eye crocodile skinks require drinking water to remain healthy. And while providing drinking water is a fairly straightforward task, there are a few things to keep in mind while doing so.

Providing Drinking Water

Unlike many other lizards who do not seem to recognize water unless it is moving, red-eye crocodile skinks readily drink standing water, so you'll want to provide your pet with a dish full of clean, fresh drinking water at all times.

While it is acceptable to offer your pet a bowl that will accommodate his entire body, it is not necessary. A 2- to 3-inch-diameter dish is big enough in most cases. Be sure to avoid filling large containers too high, as they are apt to overflow if the lizard crawls into the bowl.

Be sure to check the water dish daily and ensure that the water is clean. Empty, wash and refill the water dish any time it becomes contaminated with substrate, shed skin, urates or feces.

Some keepers prefer to use dechlorinated or bottled water for their reptiles; however, untreated tap water is used by many keepers with no ill effects.

Maintaining Proper Habitat Humidity

Red-eye crocodile skinks require fairly humid enclosures to thrive. Generally speaking, you'll want to shoot for a relative humidity of at least 70% during the day, although the humidity level can be allowed to drop at night.

To maintain a high humidity level, you'll need to periodically add water to the habitat to replace that which is lost as the air in the habitat mingles with the air in the surrounding room.

You can do so in a number of ways, but the easiest way to do so is by misting the habitat every day with room-temperature water. Be sure to spray down the sides of the enclosure as well as the substrate when doing so.

You can also pour water into the substrate if you like, but you'll need to make sure you don't add too much. Otherwise, you may flood the bottom of the habitat, which can lead to bacterial and fungal growth.

Chapter 14: Interacting with Your Red-Eye Crocodile Skink

Red-eye crocodile skinks are easy to handle, but they rarely enjoy the experience. Most would prefer to be left alone, as handling appears to stress them significantly.

Additionally, while they aren't very likely to bite the hand that holds them, they will often struggle and squirm to escape. Some may even emit vocalizations that can startle the keeper. Both behaviors may cause you to drop your lizard, which can lead to serious injuries.

However, it will occasionally be necessary to handle your pet from time to time. Accordingly, you'll need to learn the best ways to do so.

Handling a Red-Eye Crocodile Skink

The very best way to handle your red-eye crocodile skink is to allow him to walk on your outstretched hands, rather than physically restraining him. However, you may need to grip him gently but tightly, if you need to examine him closely.

To pick up your pet, try to slide a finger (or two, if the individual is large) underneath the lizard's chin. Gently apply upward pressure, and the lizard will usually begin moving up your hand or finger. Keep lifting up gently and the lizard may crawl right into your hand voluntarily.

Always be patient when transferring a red-eye crocodile skink to or from your hands. Try to "encourage" rather than "force" movements. Sometimes, tickling your lizard's foot or tail lightly will stimulate them to move more quickly.

Obviously, great care must be taken with regard to the animal's tail, which may break off if the animal becomes frightened. In general, you should avoid contact with the tail as much as is possible.

In the Event of a Bite

Red-eye crocodile skink bites are rare and amount to little more than a strong pinch when they do occur (particularly savage bites may also cause small lacerations). However, you should be prepared for the possibility, and understand the best course of action to take.

In the event of a bite, try to remain calm. Usually a frightened crocodile skink will release its bite fairly quickly. If he does not release his bite quickly, you can simply move him into his habitat, and place his feet on the ground – he'll usually let go once he feels that he can escape.

If that doesn't work, you can try placing your hand under some cool, running water, which will normally cause him to let go.

Wash all bites with soap and warm water and consult your doctor if the bite breaks the skin.

Transporting Your Pet

Although you should strive to avoid any unnecessary travel with your lizard, circumstances often demand that you do (such as when your lizard becomes ill).

Strive to make the journey as stress-free as possible for your pet. This means protecting him from physical harm, as well as blocking as much stressful stimuli as possible.

The best type of container to use when transporting your lizard is a plastic storage box. Add several ventilation holes to plastic containers to provide suitable ventilation.

Add a few paper towel tubes to the container so your pet can hide and feel secure while traveling. Place a few paper towels or some clean newspaper in the bottom of the box to absorb any fluids, should your lizard defecate or discharge urates.

Monitor your lizard regularly but avoid constantly opening the container to take a peak. Checking up on your pet once every half-hour or so is more than sufficient.

Pay special attention to the enclosure temperatures while traveling. Use your digital thermometer to monitor the air temperatures inside the transportation container. Try to keep the temperatures in the low-70s Fahrenheit (21 to 22 degrees Celsius) so that your pet will remain comfortable. Use the air-conditioning or heater in your vehicle as needed to keep the animal within this range.

Keep your skink's transportation container as stable as possible while traveling. Do not jostle your pet unnecessarily and always use a gentle touch when moving the container. Never leave the container unattended.

Because you cannot control the thermal environment, it is not wise to take your lizard with you on public transportation.

Hygiene

Reptiles can carry *Salmonella* spp., *Escherichia coli* and several other zoonotic pathogens and parasites. Accordingly, it is imperative to use good hygiene practices when handling reptiles. Always wash your hands with soap and warm water each time you touch your pet, his habitat or the tools you use to care for him. Antibacterial soaps are preferred, but standard hand soap will suffice.

In addition to keeping your hands clean, you must also take steps to ensure your environment does not become contaminated with pathogens. In general, this means keeping your skink and any of the tools and equipment you use to maintain his habitat separated from your belongings.

Establish a safe place to prepare your pet's food, store equipment and clean his habitat. Make sure the place is far from places human food is prepared. Never wash cages or tools in kitchens or bathrooms that are used by humans. Always clean and sterilize any items that become contaminated by the germs from your red-eye crocodile skink or his habitat.

Chapter 15: Common Health Concerns

Like many other reptiles, red-eye crocodile skinks are hardy animals, who often remain healthy despite their keeper's mistakes. In fact, most illnesses that befall pet red-eye crocodile skinks result from improper husbandry, and are, therefore, entirely avoidable.

Nevertheless, like most other reptiles, red-eye crocodile skinks often fail to exhibit any symptoms that they are sick until they have reached an advanced state of illness. This means that prompt action is necessary at the first hint of a problem. Doing so provides your pet with the greatest chance of recovery.

While proper husbandry is solely in the domain of the keeper, and some minor injuries or illnesses can be treated at home, veterinary care is necessary for many health problems.

Finding a Suitable Vet

While any veterinarian – even one who specializes in dogs and cats – may be able to help you keep your pet happy, it is wise to find a veterinarian who specializes in treating reptiles. Such veterinarians are more likely to be familiar with your pet species and be familiar with the most current treatment standards for reptiles.

Some of the best places to begin your search for a reptile-oriented veterinarian include:

- Veterinary associations

- Local pet stores

- Local colleges and universities

It is always wise to develop a relationship with a qualified veterinarian before you need his or her services. This way, you will already know where to go in the event of an emergency, and your veterinarian will have developed some familiarity with your pet.

When to See the Vet

Most conscientious keepers will not hesitate to seek veterinary attention on behalf of their pet. However, veterinary care can be expensive for the keeper and stressful for the kept, so unnecessary visits are best avoided.

If you are in doubt, call or email your veterinarian and explain the problem. He or she can then advise you if the problem requires an office visit or not.

However, you must always seek prompt veterinary care if your pet exhibits any of the following signs or symptoms:

- Traumatic injuries, such as lacerations, burns, broken bones or puncture wounds

- Sores, ulcers, lumps or other deformations of the skin

- Intestinal disturbances that do not resolve within 48 hours

- Drastic change in behavior

- Inability to deposit eggs

Remember that reptiles are perfectly capable of feeling pain and suffering, so apply the golden rule: If you would appreciate medical care for an injury or illness, it is likely that your pet does as well.

Common Health Problems

The following are some of the most common health problems that afflict red-eye crocodile skinks. Be alert for any signs of the following maladies and take steps to remedy the problem.

Respiratory Infections

Respiratory infections are some of the most common illnesses that afflict red-eye crocodile skinks and other captive reptiles.

The most common symptoms of respiratory infections are discharges from the nose or mouth; however, lethargy, inappetence and behavioral changes (such as basking more often than normal) may also accompany respiratory infections.

Myriad causes can lead to this type of illness, including communicable pathogens, as well as, ubiquitous, yet normally harmless, pathogens, which opportunistically infect stressed animals.

Your red-eye crocodile skink may be able to fight off these infections without veterinary assistance, but it is wise to solicit your vet's opinion at the first sign of illness. Some respiratory infections can prove fatal and require immediate attention.

Your vet will likely obtain samples, send off the samples for laboratory testing and then interpret the results. Antibiotics or other medications may be prescribed to help your red-eye crocodile skink recover, and your veterinarian will likely encourage you to keep the pet's stress level low and ensure his enclosure temperatures are ideal.

In fact, it is usually a good idea to raise the temperature of the basking spot upon first suspecting that your red-eye crocodile skink is suffering from a respiratory infection. Elevated body temperatures (such as those that occur when mammals have fevers) help the pet's body to fight the infection, and many will bask for longer than normal when ill.

Internal Parasites

In the wild, most reptiles carry some internal parasites. While it may not be possible to keep a lizard completely free of internal parasites, it is important to keep these levels in check.

Consider any wild-caught skink to be parasitized until proven otherwise. While most captive bred lizards should have relatively few internal parasites, they can suffer from such problems as well.

Most internal parasites that are of importance for red-eye crocodile skinks are transmitted via the fecal-oral route. This means that eggs (or similar life stages) of the parasites are released with the feces. If the lizard inadvertently ingests these, the resulting parasites can develop inside the lizard's body and cause illness.

Such eggs are usually microscopic and easily lifted into the air, where they may stick to cage walls or land in the water dish. Later, when the lizard flicks its tongue or drinks from the water dish, it ingests the eggs.

Because cages that are continuously contaminated from feces are likely to lead to dangerous parasite loads, employ strict hygiene practices at all times.

Internal parasites may cause your pet to vomit, pass loose stools, fail to grow or refuse food entirely. Other parasites may produce no symptoms at all, which illustrates the importance of routine examinations.

Your veterinarian will usually examine your lizard's feces if he suspects internal parasites. By looking at the type of eggs inside the lizard's feces, you veterinarian can determine which medication will treat the problem.

Many parasites are easily treated with anti-parasitic medications, but often, these medications must be given several times to eradicate the pathogens completely.

Some parasites may be transmissible to people, so always take proper precautions, including regular hand washing and keeping reptiles and their cages away from kitchens and other areas where foods are prepared.

Examples of common internal parasites include roundworms, tapeworms and amoebas.

"Mouth Rot"
Mouth rot – properly called stomatitis – can be identified by noting discoloration, discharge or cheesy-looking material in your red-eye crocodile skink's mouth. Mouth rot can be a serious illness and requires the attention of your veterinarian.

While mouth rot often follows injury (such as happens when a lizard runs into the side of a glass cage) it can also arise from systemic illness. Your veterinarian will cleanse your pet's mouth and potentially prescribe an antibiotic.

Your veterinarian may recommend withholding food until the problem is remedied. Always be sure that lizards that are recovering from mouth rot are kept in immaculately clean habitats with ideal temperature gradients.

External Parasites
The primary external parasites that afflict lizards are ticks and snake mites. Ticks are rare on captive bred animals, but wild

caught reptiles may be plagued by dozens of the small arachnids.

Ticks should be removed manually. Using tweezers grasp the tick as close as possible to the skink's skin and pull with steady, gentle pressure. Do not place anything over the tick first, such as petroleum jelly, or carry out any other "home remedies," such as burning the tick with a match. Such techniques may cause the tick to inject more saliva (which may contain diseases or bacteria) into your pet's body.

Drop the tick in a jar of isopropyl alcohol to kill it. It is a good idea to bring these to your veterinarian for analysis. Do not contact ticks with your bare hands, as many species can transmit disease to humans.

Mites are another matter entirely. While ticks are generally large enough to see easily, mites are about the size of a pepper flake. Whereas very bad tick infestations number in the dozens, mite infestations may include thousands of individual parasites.

Mites may afflict wild caught lizards, but, as they are not confined to a small cage, such infestations are somewhat self-limiting. In captivity, mite infestations can approach plague proportions.

After a female mite feeds on a lizard (or snake), she drops off and finds a safe place (such as a tiny crack in a cage or among the substrate) to deposit her eggs. After the eggs hatch, they travel back to your pet (or to other reptiles in your collection) where they feed and perpetuate the lifecycle.

Whereas a few mites may represent little more than an inconvenience to the lizard, significant infestations can stress them considerably. In extreme cases, they may even lead to anemia and eventual death. This is particularly true for small or young animals. Additionally, mites may transmit disease from one reptile to another.

There are a number of different methods for eradicating a mite infestation. In each case, there are two primary steps that must be taken: You must eradicate the lizard's parasites and eradicate the parasites in the environment (which includes the room in which the cage resides).

It is relatively simple to remove mites from a reptile. When mites get wet, they die. However, mites are protected by a thick, waxy exoskeleton that stimulates the formation of an air bubble.

To defeat this waxy cuticle, you can simply add a few drops of liquid soap to the water. The soap will lower the surface tension of water, thereby preventing the air bubble from forming.

Soaking your lizard is the slightly soapy water for about one hour will kill most of the mites on his body. Use care when doing so but try to arrange the water level and container so that most of the skink's body is below the water.

While your pet is soaking, perform a thorough cage cleaning. Remove everything from the cage, including water dishes, substrates and cage props. Sterilize all impermeable cage items and discard the substrate and all porous cage props. Vacuum the area around the cage and wipe down all of the nearby surfaces with a wet cloth.

It may be necessary to repeat this process several times to eradicate the mites completely. Accordingly, the very best strategy is to avoid contracting mites in the first place. This is why it is important to purchase your reptile from a reliable breeder or retailer, and keep it quarantined from potential mite vectors.

Even if you purchase your lizard from a reliable source, provide excellent husbandry and clean the cage regularly, you can end up battling mites if your friend brings his snake or lizard – which has a few mites – to your house.

It may even be possible for mites to crawl onto your hands or clothes, hop off when you return home and make their way to your pet.

Make it a practice to inspect your lizard and his cage regularly. Look in the crease under the animal's lower jaw, near the eyes and near the vent -- common places in which mites hide. It can also be helpful to wipe down your skink with a damp, white paper towel. After wiping down the animal, observe the towel to see if any mites are present.

Chemical treatments are also available to combat mites, but you must be very careful with such substances. Beginners should rely on their veterinarian to prescribe or suggest the appropriate products to use.

Avoid repurposing lice treatments or other chemicals, as is often encouraged by other hobbyists. Such non-intended use may be very dangerous, and it is often in violation of Federal laws.

New hobbyists should consult with their veterinarian if they suspect that their pet has mites. Mite eradication is often a challenging ordeal that your veterinarian can help make easier.

Injuries
Red-eye crocodile skinks can become injured in myriad ways. While they are likely to heal from most minor wounds

without medical attention, serious wounds will necessitate veterinary assistance.

Your vet will likely clean the wound, make any repairs necessary and prescribe a course of antibiotics to help prevent infection. Be sure to keep the enclosure as clean as possible during the healing process.

Egg Binding
Egg binding occurs when a female is unable or unwilling to deposit her eggs in a timely fashion. If not treated promptly, death can result.

The primary symptoms of egg binding are similar to those that occur when a gravid red-eye crocodile skink approaches parturition. Egg bound red-eye crocodile skinks may explore their egg deposition chamber incessantly or attempt to escape their enclosure. However, unlike reptiles who will deposit eggs normally, egg bound red-eye crocodile skinks continue to exhibit these symptoms without producing a clutch of eggs.

As long as you are expecting your red-eye crocodile skink to lay eggs, you can easily monitor her behavior and act quickly if she experiences problems. However, if you are not anticipating a clutch, this type of problem can catch you by surprise.

Prolapse
Prolapses occur when a red-eye crocodile skink's intestines protrude from its vent. This is an emergency situation that requires prompt treatment. Fortunately, intestinal prolapse is not terribly common among red-eye crocodile skinks.

You will need to take the animal to the veterinarian, who will attempt to re-insert the intestinal sections. Sometimes sutures will be necessary to keep the intestines in place while the muscles regain their tone.

Try to keep the exposed tissue damp, clean and protected while traveling to the vet. It is likely that this problem is very painful for the animal, so try to keep its stress level low during the process.

Quarantine

Quarantine is the practice of isolating animals to prevent them from transferring diseases between themselves.

If you have no other pet reptiles (particularly other red-eye crocodile skinks), quarantine is unnecessary. However, if you already maintain other red-eye crocodile skinks you must provide all new acquisitions with a separate enclosure.

At a minimum, quarantine all new acquisitions for 30 days. However, it is wiser still to extend the quarantine period for 60 to 90 days, to give yourself a better chance of discovering any illness present before exposing your colony to new, potentially sick, animals. Professional zoological institutions often quarantine animals for six months to a year. In fact, some zoos keep their animals in a state of perpetual quarantine.

Chapter 16: Breeding Red-Eye Crocodile Skinks

Many reptile keepers are intrigued at the idea of breeding their pets. While this is a fun, educational activity, you must be sure that you understand the risks and responsibilities that accompany such attempts.

For example, males may suffer damaged hemipenes and females may become egg bound. Either of which may be fatal without prompt treatment. You may find it necessary to take your pet to the veterinarian for costly treatment – potentially without any guarantee of success.

If you manage to get through the entire process without problem, you will one day find eggs that require incubation. If this is successful, you will find yourself caring for many more red-eye crocodile skinks. While it is possible to sell them, this is not as easy as it sounds, and rarely generates profit.

Many municipalities require expensive permits to keep large numbers of reptiles – selling them requires other permits altogether. You will have to learn how to ship red-eye crocodile skinks and obtain the necessary permits for that.

Additionally, you will have to spend money to advertise that you have lizards for sale. Ultimately, most beginners find that it is simply best to give away their red-eye crocodile skinks to other keepers.

Finally, you must consider the costs associated with housing a large number of hatchlings. Each will need its own food supply and perhaps its own cage.

Pre-Cycling Conditioning

Only red-eye crocodile skinks in perfect health should be considered for breeding trials. If a lizard exhibits signs of stress, respiratory illness, mites, mouth rot or other illnesses, avoid breeding the animal until it is 100 percent health.

Prior to breeding season, you'll need to feed adults slated for breeding trials heavily. However, avoid allowing either animal to become overweight – overweight red-eye crocodile skinks make poor breeders.

Cycling

While many reptiles require their keepers to implement a cycling regimen, which mimics the seasonal changes that occur in the animals' native lands, red-eye crocodile skinks do not appear to require drastic environmental changes to breed successfully.

The temperatures in New Guinea remain relatively consistent throughout the year, so this makes sense. However, the amount of rainfall that occurs in the red-eye crocodile skink's native lands does change throughout the year. Although the island receives a significant amount of rainfall throughout the year, the rainfall is quite heavy between the months of November and March.

This rainy season coincides with the breeding season for red-eye crocodile skinks, so many keepers try to recreate a rainy season for their captives.

To recreate the rainy season, most keepers simply try to mist the habitat heavily for several weeks. It may be necessary to mist the habitat twice a day (instead of the normal rate of once per day) to adequately recreate a "wet season."

Breeding will often occur shortly after increasing the misting frequency, but it can be difficult to know for sure, thanks to the secretive nature of red-eye crocodile skinks.

Pairing

Most keepers maintain red-eye crocodile skinks together as a matter of practice, so this alleviates the need to pair them up during the breeding season.

However, some keepers do prefer to keep the sexes separately throughout the year, and only introduce them to each other during breeding attempts.

It is always wise to observe red-eye crocodile skinks when you introduce them to each other – particularly when it is the first time two have met. Some lizards just are not compatible, and may engage in antagonistic behaviors or fight. This can lead to serious injuries or death if the subordinate animal cannot escape.

Some breeders prefer to place males in the females' cages, while others prefer the opposite. Still others use a neutral cage, unique to both.

Pairs may begin copulating minutes after you place them in the same cage, or they may never breed if they are not compatible. Generally, you'll want to place your red-eye crocodile skinks together for several weeks to ensure the best chances of fertile matings.

Egg Deposition and Post-Partum Care

After several weeks of being housed together, the female can be separated. You'll want to feed her heavily to help prepare her for the rigors of gestation and egg depositions. However, you must always offer smaller-than-normal food items at this time, to reduce the chances of disrupting the reproductive processes.

Most red-eye crocodile skinks will bury their eggs in the substrate, so egg-laying boxes are not required. Once you discover an egg, you'll want to carefully remove it and place it in an incubator.

You probably won't notice the female depositing the eggs, but if you do, you'll want to take very good care of her during this time.

Allow the female to rest and rehydrate for about 24 hours, and then offer her food. Most females eat ravenously at this time to help replenish their energy stores.

The Incubator
You can either purchase a commercially produced incubator or construct your own. However, most beginning breeders are better served by purchasing a commercial incubator than making their own.

Commercial Incubators
Commercial egg incubators come in myriad styles and sizes. Some of the most popular models are similar to those used to incubate poultry eggs (these are often available for purchase from livestock supply retailers).

These incubators are constructed from a large foam box, fitted with a heating element and thermostat. Some models feature a fan for circulating air; while helpful for maintaining a uniform thermal environment, models that lack these fans are acceptable.

You can place an incubation medium directly in the bottom of these types of incubators, although it is preferable to place the media (and eggs) inside small plastic storage boxes, which are then placed inside the incubator.

These incubators are usually affordable and easy to use, although their foam-based construction makes them less durable than most premium incubators are.

Other incubators are constructed from metal or plastic boxes; feature a clear door, an enclosed heating element and a thermostat. Some units also feature a backup thermostat, which can provide some additional protection in case the primary thermostat fails.

These types of incubators usually outperform economy, foam-based models, but they also bear higher price tags. Either style will work, but, if you plan to breed red-eye crocodile skinks for many years, premium models usually present the best option.

Homemade Incubators

Although incubators can be constructed in a variety of ways, using many different materials and designs, two basic designs are most common.

The first type of homemade incubator consists of a plastic, glass or wood box, and a simple heat source, such as a piece of heat tape or a low-wattage heat lamp. The heating source must be attached to a thermostat to keep the temperatures consistent. A thermometer is also necessary for monitoring the temperatures of the incubator.

Some keepers make these types of incubators from wood, while others prefer plastic or foam. Although glass is a poor insulator, aquariums often serve as acceptable incubators; however, you must purchase or construct a solid top to retain heat.

Place a brick on the bottom of the incubator, and place the egg box on top of the brick, so that the eggs are not resting directly on the heat tape. The brick will also provide thermal mass to the incubator, which will help maintain a more consistent temperature.

The other popular incubator design adds a quantity of water to the design to help maintain consistent temperatures and a higher humidity. To build such a unit, begin with an aquarium fitted with a glass or plastic lid.

Place a brick in the bottom of the aquarium and add about two gallons of water to the aquarium; ideally, the water level should stop right below the top of the brick.

Add an aquarium heater to the water and set the thermostat to the desired temperature. Place the egg box on the brick, insert a temperature probe into the egg box and cover the aquarium with the lid (you may need to purchase a lid designed to allow the cords to pass through it).

This type of incubator works by heating the water, which will in turn heat the air inside the incubator, which will heat the eggs. Although it can take several days of repeated adjustments to get these types of incubators set to the exact temperature you would like, they are very stable once established.

Incubation

Most breeders incubate red-eye crocodile skinks eggs inside small plastic boxes containing an incubation medium. The boxes are then placed inside the incubation chamber.

A thermostat keeps the temperature correct, while the humidity of the box is controlled by adding water to the substrate as needed.

Plastic storage boxes are often used for egg incubation. Fill the box half way with damp vermiculite. Ensure that the vermiculite is damp enough to clump, but not so damp that it drips when compressed. As a starting point, combine equal weights of water and vermiculite and then adjust the mixture as necessary. Make a few small holes in the incubation box to provide some air exchange.

Before removing the eggs from the egg-laying box, mark the top of each egg with a graphite pencil. This is necessary because the tiny lizard embryo attaches to the inside of the eggshell at an early stage in development. If the egg is rotated after this happens, the young animal can drown inside the egg.

After marking the tops, gently remove the eggs and transfer them to the egg incubation box. Do not use force to separate any eggs that are attached – while experienced breeders often separate such eggs, the risk of destroying some of them is high. Simply place clumps of attached eggs in the egg incubation box in the same orientation in which they are in the deposition box.

Place the eggs in the incubation box in the same orientation in which they were deposited in the egg-laying box. Bury the eggs about halfway in the vermiculite.

There are many different opinions regarding the best place to install the thermostat's temperature probe. Some prefer placing it in the main incubator chamber, while others prefer to place the probe inside the egg box.

Place the egg incubation box inside the incubator and close it tightly. Do not inspect the eggs too frequently, as this may cause unnecessary temperature spikes.

Red-eye crocodile skink eggs typically take about 70 days to complete their development. You can incubate the eggs at about 78 degrees Fahrenheit (25 degrees Celsius).

Hatchling Husbandry

Establish "nursery cages" for the young red-eye crocodile skinks about a week before the eggs should hatch. The container should contain only a paper towel substrate, a very shallow water dish and a few places to hide (crumpled newspaper works well).

Keep the nursery very clean, slightly humid and at about 75 degrees Fahrenheit (24 degrees Celsius), 24-hours a day. The hatchlings do not need much light – that coming in the side of the nursery is ample. Do not handle the hatchlings unless necessary, until they are about one month old and eating well.

It is not uncommon for hatchlings to emerge with their yolks still attached. Do not attempt to remove or separate the tissue in such situations; doing so could cause severe injury or death to the hatchling. Instead, simply keep the hatchling in a nursery cage and ensure that the tissue does not dry out. Generally, by keeping the nursery slightly humid, the tissue will remain moist and dethatch on in its own in a few days.

Hatchlings are usually ready to be placed in their permanent enclosures within a few weeks. At this point, you can place them in habitats that are like small versions of the adult cages.

Give them a few days to settle in and begin offering food.

Chapter 17: Further Reading

Never stop learning more about your new pet's natural history, biology and captive care. This is the only way to ensure that you are providing your new lizard with the highest quality of life possible.

It's always more fun to watch your red-eye crocodile skink than to read about him, but by accumulating more knowledge, you'll be better able to provide him with a high quality of life.

Note: at the time of printing, all the websites below were working. As the internet changes rapidly, some sites might no longer be live when you read this book. That is, of course, out of our control.

Books

Bookstores and online book retailers offer a treasure trove of information that will advance your quest for knowledge. While books represent an additional cost involved in reptile care, you can consider it an investment in your pet's well-being. Your local library may also carry some books about red-eye crocodile skinks, which you can borrow for no charge.

University libraries are a great place for finding old, obscure or academically oriented books about red-eye crocodile skinks. You may not be allowed to borrow these books if you are not a student, but you can view and read them at the library.

Herpetology: An Introductory Biology of Amphibians and Reptiles
By Laurie J. Vitt, Janalee P. Caldwell
Top of Form
Bottom of Form

Academic Press, 2013

Understanding Reptile Parasites: A Basic Manual for Herpetoculturists & Veterinarians
By Roger Klingenberg D.V.M.
Advanced Vivarium Systems, 1997

Infectious Diseases and Pathology of Reptiles: Color Atlas and Text
Elliott Jacobson
CRC Press

Designer Reptiles and Amphibians
Richard D. Bartlett, Patricia Bartlett
Barron's Educational Series

Magazines

Because magazines are typically published monthly or bi-monthly, they occasionally offer more up-to-date information than books do. Magazine articles are obviously not as comprehensive as books typically are, but they still have considerable value.

Reptiles Magazine
www.reptilesmagazine.com/
Covering reptiles commonly kept in captivity.

Practical Reptile Keeping
http://www.practicalreptilekeeping.co.uk/
Practical Reptile Keeping is a popular publication aimed at beginning and advanced hobbies. Topics include the care and maintenance of popular reptiles as well as information on wild reptiles.

Websites

The internet has made it much easier to find information about reptiles than it has ever been.

However, you must use discretion when deciding which websites to trust. While knowledgeable breeders, keepers and academics operate some websites, many who maintain reptile-oriented websites lack the same dedication to scientific rigor.

Anyone with a computer and internet connection can launch a website and say virtually anything they want about red-eye crocodile skinks. Accordingly, as with all other research, consider the source of the information before making any husbandry decisions.

The Reptile Report
www.thereptilereport.com/
The Reptile Report is a news-aggregating website that accumulates interesting stories and features about reptiles from around the world.

Kingsnake.com
www.kingsnake.com
After starting as a small website for gray-banded kingsnake enthusiasts, Kingsnake.com has become one of the largest reptile-oriented portals in the hobby. The site features classified advertisements, a breeder directory, message forums and other resources.

The Vivarium and Aquarium News

www.vivariumnews.com/
The online version of the former print publication, The Vivarium and Aquarium News provides in-depth coverage of

different reptiles and amphibians in a captive and wild context.

Journals

Journals are the primary place professional scientists turn when they need to learn about red-eye crocodile skinks. While they may not make light reading, hobbyists stand to learn a great deal from journals.

Herpetologica
www.hljournals.org/
Published by The Herpetologists' League, Herpetologica, and its companion publication, Herpetological Monographs cover all aspects of reptile and amphibian research.

Journal of Herpetology
www.ssarherps.org/
Produced by the Society for the Study of Reptiles and Amphibians, the Journal of Herpetology is a peer-reviewed publication covering a variety of reptile-related topics.

Copeia
www.asihcopeiaonline.org/
Copeia is published by the American Society of Ichthyologists and Herpetologists. A peer-reviewed journal, Copeia covers all aspects of the biology of reptiles, amphibians and fish.

Nature
www.nature.com/
Although Nature covers all aspects of the natural world, many issues contain information that red-eye crocodile skink enthusiasts are sure to find interesting.

Supplies

You can obtain most of what you need to maintain red-eye crocodile skinks through your local pet store, big-box retailer or hardware store, but online retailers offer another option.

Just be sure that you consider the shipping costs for any purchase, to ensure you aren't "saving" yourself a few dollars on the product yet spending several more dollars to get the product delivered.

Big Apple Pet Supply
http://www.bigappleherp.com
Big Apple Pet Supply carries most common husbandry equipment, including heating devices, water dishes and substrates.

LLLReptile
http://www.lllreptile.com
LLL Reptile carries a wide variety of husbandry tools, heating devices, lighting products and more.

Doctors Foster and Smith
http://www.drsfostersmith.com
Foster and Smith is a veterinarian-owned retailer that supplies husbandry-related items to pet keepers.

Support Organizations

Sometimes, the best way to learn about red-eye crocodile skinks is to reach out to other keepers and breeders. Check out these organizations, and search for others in your geographic area.

The National Reptile & Amphibian Advisory Council

http://www.nraac.org/

The National Reptile & Amphibian Advisory Council seeks to educate the hobbyists, legislators and the public about reptile and amphibian related issues.

American Veterinary Medical Association

www.avma.org

The AVMA is a good place for Americans to turn if you are having trouble finding a suitable reptile veterinarian.

The World Veterinary Association

http://www.worldvet.org/

The World Veterinary Association is a good resource for finding suitable reptile veterinarians worldwide.

References

Almeida, M. L.-R.-F. (2006). Distribution of neuromuscular junctions in laryngeal and syringeal muscles in vertebrates.

Anderson, S. P. (2003). The Phylogenetic Definition of Reptilia. *Systematic Biology*.

Antonieta Labra, G. S. (2013). Acoustic Features of the Weeping Lizard's Distress Call. *Copeia*.

AUSTIN, C. C. (2006). Checklist and Comments on the Terrestrial Reptile Fauna of Kau Wildlife Area, Papua New Guinea. *Herpetological Review*.

Bergmann, P. J. (2008). A phylogenetic and functional approach to the study of the evolution of body shape in lizards (Squamata). *University of Massachusetts Amherst*.

Bruce A. Young, N. M. (2013). Reptile Auditory Neuroethology: What Do Reptiles Do with Their Hearing? *Insights from Comparative Hearing Research*.

Christopher C. Austin, E. N. (2010). Phylogeny, historical biogeography and body size evolution in Pacific Island Crocodile skinks Tribolonotus (Squamata; Scincidae). *Molecular Phylogenetics and Evolution*.

Cogger, H. (1972). A new scincid lizard of the genus Tribolonotus from Manus Island, New Guinea. *Zoologische Mededelingen*.

Donnellan, S. C. (1991). Chromosomes of Australian lygosomine &inks (Lacertilia: Scincidae) . *Genetica*.

Hartdegen, R. W., Russell, M. J., Young, B., & Reams, R. D. (2002). Vocalization and parental care of Tribolonotus gracilis. *Herpetological Review*.

R. Michael Burger, W. H. (2007). Evaluation of UVB reduction by materials commonly used in reptile husbandry. *Zoo Biology*.

Sam R. Telford, J. a. (2005). TWO PLASMODIUM SPECIES OF THE CROCODILE SKINK TRIBOLONOTUS GRACILIS FROM IRIAN JAYA, INDONESIA. *Journal of Parasitology* .

Thornton, S. C. (2003). Colonization of an island volcano, Long Island, Papua New Guinea, and an emergent island, Motmot, in its caldera lake. IV. Colonization by non-avian vertebrates. *Journal of Biogeography*.

W.Reeder, T. (2003). A phylogeny of the Australian Sphenomorphus group (Scincidae: Squamata) and the phylogenetic placement of the crocodile skinks (Tribolonotus): Bayesian approaches to assessing congruence and obtaining confidence in maximum likelihood inferred relationship. *Molecular Phylogenetics and Evolution*.

Wurst, G. C. (1976). The Occurrence of Parietal Eyes in Recent Lacertilia (Reptilia). *Journal of Herpetology*.

ZWEIFEL, R. G. (1966). A New Lizard of the Genus Tribolonotus (Scincidae) from New Britain. *American Museum Novitates*.

Index

Made in the USA
Las Vegas, NV
26 January 2022

42303973R00066